ALCTS Papers on Library Technical Services and Collections, no. 8

Virtually Yours

Models for Managing Electronic Resources and Services

---

*Proceedings of the Joint
Reference and User Services Association
and
Association for Library Collections
and Technical Services Institute*

*Chicago, Illinois
October 23–25, 1997*

edited by

Peggy Johnson and Bonnie MacEwan

*American Library Association
Chicago and London
1999*

While extensive effort has gone into ensuring the reliability of information appearing in this book, the publisher makes no warranty, express or implied, on the accuracy or reliability of the information, and does not assume and hereby disclaims any liability to any person for any loss or damage caused by errors or omissions in this publication.

Project editor: Louise D. Howe

Cover design: Dianne M. Rooney

Composition by the dotted i in Times and Helvetica Narrow using QuarkXPress 3.32

Printed on 50-pound Windsor Offset, a pH-neutral stock, and bound in 10-point coated cover stock by McNaughton & Gunn

The paper used in this publication meets the minimum requirements of American National Standard for Information Sciences—Permanence of Paper for Printed Library Materials, ANSI Z39.48-1992. ♾

Library of Congress Cataloging-in-Publication Data

Virtually yours : models for managing electronic resources and services / edited by Peggy Johnson and Bonnie MacEwan ; with the Association for Library Collections & Technical Services and the Reference & User Services Association.
     p.   cm. — (ALCTS papers on library technical services and collections ; no. 8)
    Papers from a joint institute held Oct. 23–25, 1997 in Chicago, Ill.
    Includes bibliographical references and index.
    ISBN 0-8389-0753-9
    1. Libraries—United States—Special collections—Electronic information resources.
I. Johnson, Peggy, 1948– . II. MacEwan, Bonnie. III. Association for Library Collections & Technical Services. IV. Reference and User Services Association. V. Series.
Z692.C65V57   1998
025.17′4—dc21   98-41982

Printed in the United States of America.

03   02   01   00   99   5   4   3   2   1

Contents

Preface

"Virtually Yours: Models for Managing Electronic Resources and Services," the Joint Reference and User Services Association (RUSA) and the Association for Library Collections and Technical Services (ALCTS) Institute, was held at the Ambassador West Hotel in Chicago, October 23–25, 1997. This was the first joint institute, following the successful Advanced Collection Management and Development Institute[1] sponsored by the Collection Management and Development Section of ALCTS of the American Library Association.

Many people were involved in developing this joint institute. David Farrell, University of California/Berkeley, initiated planning, expanding on a proposal for a second advanced collection management and development institute developed by Gay Dannelly, Ohio State University, and Bonnie MacEwan, Pennsylvania State University. Cindy Kaag, Washington State University, and Barbara Allen, Committee on Institutional Cooperation, served as cochairs of the joint institute planning committee. Other librarians who helped organize the institute included Suzanne Fedunok, New York University; Peggy Johnson, University of Minnesota; Bonnie MacEwan, Pennsylvania State University; Kathleen Sullivan, Thousand Oaks Library (California); Diane Zabel, Pennsylvania State University; and Eugene Wiemers, Bates College. Yvonne McLean and Karen Whittlesey from the ALCTS staff provided professional support and liaison for conference arrangement.

The idea for this institute built on a long tradition of ALCTS institutes focusing on collections, dating back to the first Regional Collection Management and Development Institute in 1981. As planners began to develop the second advanced institute, they saw a need to span the boundaries that have defined collection management and development theory in the past twenty years. To this end, RUSA jointly sponsored and developed all aspects of this new institute. The planning committee's intent was a new focus on the convergence of collections and services experienced as libraries move into an increasingly digital environment.

This joint RUSA/ALCTS Institute was designed to explore the reconceptualization of collection development and public services and the changes that electronic resources and access are bringing for users, services, and collections. The institute's goals were to (1) identify positive models for the role of collection development and public services staffs in changing environments, (2) provide a forum for the discussion and exploration of these new roles, and (3) help identify personal and organizational goals to affect appropriate change in response to these new environments.

Participants met for two and a half days and heard presentations that formed the basis of the papers in this book. With one exception, the sixteen papers that comprise this book were presented at the Institute. The editors prepared the first chapter for this volume to provide a context for the papers, drawing on the remarks Barbara Allen prepared for the Institute's conclusion. Cindy Kaag prepared introductions for each speaker at the Institute; her introductions are included in this collection of the proceedings. A bibliography drawing on the papers' references and supplemented by the editors concludes the book.

This landmark joint institute broke ground by bringing together two diverse groups to plan an institute, prepare papers, and share ideas. We hope the synergy created by this coming together is reflected in the papers and that the energy of the conference is carried forward and continued by our readers, leading to further cross-specialization discussion and joint institutes.

Peggy Johnson and Bonnie MacEwan

Note

1. *Collection Management and Development: Issues in an Electronic Era,* ed. Peggy Johnson and Bonnie MacEwan (Chicago: American Library Association, 1994).

Acknowledgments

Bonnie and Peggy thank the authors, who delivered their papers in a timely fashion and only needed a little nagging. They thank Barbara Allen and Cindy Kaag, who made the ALCTS/RUSA Institute happen, each other for the friendship that survived yet another co-editing project, and their spouses (and children, in one case) for being perpetually supportive.

Introduction

Real Collections and Real Services in a Virtual World

Peggy Johnson and
Bonnie MacEwan

The convergence of services and collections driven by the development of electronic information is fostering partnerships both within libraries and where libraries and librarians intersect with those outside the library. Partnerships within the library must cross traditional functional divisions (public services, technical services, collection management and development, library automation) to provide the information resources and services expected today. External partnerships may be political (local, state, or federal government) or organizational (those who use libraries, govern the organizations of which libraries are a part, or provide the products libraries need). An increasingly important partnership must develop between libraries and the community of researchers, authors, and the publishers of information. In addition, libraries must look to partnerships with funding agencies and the corporate sector. Such affiliations should no longer be seen as simply sources of money, hardware, and software, but as mutually beneficial.

Through partnerships, librarians will be positioned to influence decision making, public policy, distribution of funds for library and information services, pricing and marketing of information resources, and information and automation products themselves. Such efforts can span the boundaries that have created divisions in the past. They are necessary to foster the dialog that is essential for creative problem solving.

To address successfully the changes and challenges libraries face and to pursue the many opportunities available through electronic information resources, librarians must begin with a clear understanding of and commitment to the fundamental mission of each individual library within its own unique context. Librarians must identify their library's users, understand their needs, and establish guidelines for the types and levels of service they can and will provide. Few library and information organizations will be able to sustain the current level of investment in traditional collections and services while aggressively pursuing development of a twenty-first century digital service model. Choices and compromises will be necessary to provide real services and real collections. All libraries will be called upon to manage their human and fiscal resources to best meet a finite set of goals and services, understanding that these goals and services will exist within mutable boundaries.

The chapters that comprise this book explore the reconceptualization of collection development and public services and the changes that electronic resources and access are bringing for users, services, and collections. They identify positive models for collection development and public services librarians in changing environments and suggest ways in which to play a leadership role in boundary-spanning activities. The authors write from their personal experiences within the context of the changes all librarians are experiencing. Their chapters are informative and thought provoking, and they provide sound, practical advice for challenging times.

The four chapters in part I, "Understanding Libraries and Their Mission," set the stage by exploring the evolving nature of libraries and the need for their missions to keep pace. Ross Atkinson addresses libraries' responsibility to redefine services explicitly to take full advantage of the opportunities inherent in the transition from traditional to digital services. He gives specific attention to the implications for access and services that changes in the nature of information ownership and delivery may bring. Atkinson's paper provides a call to action for all information specialists. He presses for clarifying goals, spanning boundaries, and taking charge of this new information environment.

Eugene Wiemers takes the reader in the direction that Atkinson advocates, seeking both to clarify the library's goals and to span organizational and service boundaries. He leads us into the library from the users' point of view and presents the users' vision of library and information service operations as a seamless whole. He stresses the importance of strong partnerships between users and the library, between the library and campus information services, and between the various divisions within the library in order to bring collections and services closer to the users' vision.

John Howe, speaking from the perspective of a faculty user, stresses the varying needs of users and cautions librarians to avoid generalizing as they define and design collections and services. While the community of users is, indeed, a community drawn together by new technologies, these very technologies provide an opportunity to offer choices that should not be ignored. Howe calls for librarians to remember "one size" does not fit all users.

Deanna Marcum cuts to the chase and reminds readers that partnerships require contributions from as well as benefits to the partners. The digital environment calls for a redefinition of cooperation between libraries and both the profit and not-for-profit sectors. Too often these relationships have been seen primarily as adversarial. Marcum encourages librarians to embrace the opportunities these partnerships can provide, realizing that both sides have much to gain within the context of their particular needs and interests.

Part II, "Understanding User Needs in a Changing Environment," explores matching libraries' capabilities with the user community's expectations. Too often, users and libraries' governing institutions have expectations that cannot yet be realized. Libraries are encouraged to distinguish between valid constraints and those created by outmoded services and collection models and obsolete organizational structures and functional boundaries. Libraries can be caught in the tension between user expectations and the library's inability to explore how to begin meeting them. Libraries are directed to work with their user communities to define a common understanding of service and collections goals and the path and time line to reach them. An increasingly important aspect of developing digital collections is the need for a library to be proactive in understanding its users.

Bonnie MacEwan returns to the theme underlined by both Atkinson and Weimers: the library must begin to redefine services and collections to take full advantage of the changing nature of information resources and to meet the changing expectations of our users in this new environment. To respond to these changes, collections and services must grow closer together and create organizational structures that respond to the interconnected nature of their responsibilities. Many of the barriers between collections, services, and other parts of the library organization are artificial in an era of virtual collections and the services that support them.

Gloriana St. Clair stresses the absolute necessity of doing program assessment in order to satisfy library users. Libraries can provide satisfaction only by knowing what users want, what they like, and what they do not like. St. Clair guides the reader through an understanding of the audiences for assessments and provides an overview of various assessment and analysis techniques. She states that one important benefit of conducting assessments is data to meet the demands of accountability. Only by effectively communicating this information to organizational leadership can libraries survive into the twenty-first century. To do otherwise places the future of libraries at serious risk.

Kenneth Dowlin provides a case study of what can happen when communication between the library and its user community and governing bodies fails. In his environmental scan, he shows how dissonance and disconnection can doom the library. Balancing a vision of the future and continuing expectations for traditional collections and services is a perpetual challenge for libraries. Part of the library's responsibility is to educate its user community about the difference between the possible and the ideal.

The chapters in part III, "Understanding 'Digital' Libraries: Practical Implications," ground the futuristic view of digital libraries in the reality of providing services and collections. As libraries implement digital collections and services, they must solve many pragmatic problems and issues. These issues are technical and legal. Providing the information and services efficiently and effectively is a challenge for all libraries. Libraries must stretch their organizational boundaries to develop the skills and expertise to meet these challenges.

Clifford Lynch calls for coherence between the expanding digitized collection and print materials. He stresses the library as an integrated whole that offers the user a seamless source of information and services. Thus, the digital library of the future is, in some ways, a misnomer. The library of the future provides the user with links between all sources of information—indexes and full-text, journal articles and monographs, numeric and textual resources, etc.—regardless of delivery mechanism. He identifies several specific technical aspects of navigating and integrating in the digital library that need attention to maximize its potential and to reduce the "noise" between users and the information they need.

The practical implications of legal issues for libraries are just as formidable and complex as the implications of new technologies. The challenges posed by the transition from purchasing print materials to licensing the rights to access digital information are some of the most complex facing librarians today. Dealing with licenses, contracts, copyright, intellectual property, distance education, accessing, content, service, users' rights along with libraries' rights can test any librarian who seeks to provide seamless library collections and services for users.

Kenneth Crews provides a legal primer, defining the key terms and concepts needed to understand digital information contracts and licenses. He states that the growth of licensing is a reminder that the law often affects the essence of libraries. Karen Schmidt expands on this idea. She provides practical advice on reviewing and implementing licenses. She stresses the importance of considering their impact on users and collections. Librarians cannot risk the consequences of a passive approach to legal issues. Trisha Davis outlines an approach to negotiating licenses that will best meet the economic and services goals of the library. She recommends building partnerships with the legal community and information providers to develop the best possible licenses—those that meet the needs of all parties and protect the rights of libraries and their users.

Part IV, "Understanding Change in Libraries: Implementation Considerations," brings the reader to the reality of coping with pervasive change. If libraries are to stretch beyond traditional boundaries to build the collections and services of the future, they must seek opportunities and identify ways to embrace change with creative results.

Kären Nagy provides a case study based on library initiatives at Stanford University. She describes three creative ventures resulting from the library's evolving vision of its mission and future. Over the last seven years, Stanford has integrated undergraduate library support into general services and created a new set of computing and instruction technology support services. Technical services has been redesigned with a resulting $750,000 cost saving. Most clearly responding to the changing information environment is HotWire Press, a Stanford University Libraries unit. HotWire is an information technology partner with scholarly society publishers to distribute their journals electronically. Stanford's experiences offer a model by demonstrating the potential of embracing the changes and challenges facing libraries.

Peggy Johnson's chapter suggests the reader step back from the immediacy of the many changes buffeting libraries and librarians and explore change as a phenomenon. This concluding piece explains the three stages of change and suggests why individuals (librarians and their community of users) find it a stressful experience. She suggests ways in which change can be managed more effectively and should be embraced as an opportunity rather than fought as a battle.

The chapters in this book raise large questions and do not provide all the answers. As technology enhances user access to information in libraries, reducing barriers of time and place, these same users are less likely to be tolerant of arbitrary boundaries. Librarians will face a number of challenges in order to provide our users with the full benefit of this shift in the nature of the information that will be available in the future. Many of those challenges have to do with the nature of the information and how users will expect to find, access, and acquire the information. Some of the challenges will be organizational in nature. The way libraries are organized internally, the way they interact with their immediate external environment, and the way they will interact with potential partners in the broader world of their work are undergoing similar changes. There is a need to understand legal terms and contracts in new and demanding ways. Finally, librarians are coping with the personal and professional changes inherent in change.

The authors of these papers issue a call to action. Librarians need to foster cooperation through partnerships and cooperation. They are called upon to

PART I

Understanding Libraries and Their Mission

1

Toward a Redefinition of Library Services

Ross Atkinson

Building two libraries simultaneously, a digital one and a traditional one, is highly problematic, especially in the absence of a major funding increase—but most libraries today have decided quite rightly to try to accept that challenge. Most libraries have made the commitment to bring about the transition from traditional to digital services. We who manage libraries are not therefore merely reacting to changes in the environment, but are rather acknowledging potential opportunities for change, which will greatly enhance access. It is important always to bear in mind, therefore, that this transition is not something being done to us, but is rather something we have chosen to do in fulfillment of our most basic service mission.

Such a transformation will necessarily entail an enhancement and redefinition of library services. My purpose in this chapter is to provide some suggestions or discussion points for that redefinition. As an academic librarian, I approach these issues primarily from the standpoint of library support to higher education and research, but I am hopeful that most of the points I make will be applicable to all types of libraries.

Parameters

We must consider at the outset the parameters of any such reassessment of library services. How far should we be prepared to go in re-visioning our purpose and operation? Should we set parameters at all? I think we must—but we should also be willing to extend such boundaries as widely as possible. I would draw the line—seriously—at the mystical-religious. On the mystical plane, the practitioner encounters the ultimate knowledge-experience: the unio-mystica, the intimate blending of the individual with the cosmos. It is the "kensho" of Zen Buddhism: the direct and unalloyed apprehension of reality. We can begin by acknowledging, therefore, that access to such a level of knowledge is obviously out of scope for information services.

At the same time, however, we must also assert that every form of knowledge up to that level of the mystical-religious does fall within the bounds of information services. This is a worthwhile distinction, because what apparently separates mystical from nonmystical knowledge is that the experience of knowledge on the nonmystical plane entails some form of mediation: there must always be something between the perceiver and the perceived. The individual never knows reality directly, but rather unavoidably perceives it always through some intermediary faculty or agent.

Disintermediation

Such dependence upon mediation nevertheless generally is distrusted and even disliked. One hankers always for direct knowledge of reality—hence the temptation and ubiquity of mysticism. One may hanker for *disintermediation,* which is the removal or reduction of the role of librarians in linking the user and information. Disintermediation did not originate in information services with the advent of computer technology—and it is precisely because of this general preference to avoid or reduce reliance upon mediation whenever possible that it is only natural for users to be interested in circumventing the library, for example, to connect more directly to information whenever practicable. At the same time, we (and certainly our users) recognize that mediation takes many forms. Some of those forms are, to be sure, positive or even essential, providing enhancement, amplification, clarification—while other forms can be intrusive. We must continuously review library services, therefore, to identify and mitigate instances of intrusive mediation.

It would be a serious error for libraries to dismiss or denigrate the trend toward disintermediation. It should not be viewed as some kind of threat or hobgoblin pursuing the library profession. We must rather understand and accept it as part of that very transition we are trying to bring about. Disintermediation is, after all, one of the primary goals of education in general. The teacher does not intend to interpose herself or himself indefinitely between the student and the subject. The aim always is to bring the student to a level at which he or she can be delivered over to the subject, in order to know and interact with it more directly. The library, as a primary vehicle of education, must come to hold similar views of disintermediation. The danger for libraries, therefore, is not that, if we do things wrong, a certain amount of disintermediation will result—but rather that a certain amount of disintermediation will not evolve, for that absence of disintermediation would ultimately prove detrimental to our users' interests. In short, we must be prepared to make disintermediation a goal of library services—but always with the understanding that, on the nonmystical plane, total disintermediation is never possible. This means that disintermediation is, in fact, always a form of re-mediation. New forms of mediation will be needed and will develop. If we in library services have the foresight and the agility—if we can move quickly enough—we can create and offer such new services.

Time

Speed is indeed the operative term, for all information services are ultimately understandable only in terms of time. Time is the currency of access: how long it takes for the user to gain access to needed materials; how long an item remains needed or relevant; how long an item can survive in its present physical form; how the time of the user can be expanded through an investment of the time of library staff—and above all, how much time the user has available to achieve a particular research goal. Users probably spend, in any event, too much time finding information—time that they should spend reading (or otherwise absorbing) it; and they probably spend too much time reading things—when they should instead be thinking. There is notoriously too much information to be read and digested effectively—and the next generation of computers, to be truly applicable to real information needs, should somehow be able to read for the user. That is not an unreasonable demand—although we must at the same time take care not to distinguish too sharply the activities of finding information, reading it, and thinking about it, for these are surely in many ways merely separate stages or methods of a single process.

Context

One of the most essential time-reduction tools provided by library services is the local collection. For purposes of this chapter, let us adopt as broad a definition of the collection as possible. Let us define a collection as any set of linked information objects. The purpose of collection development in the most traditional sense is in fact always to link specific objects—documents, publications—by moving them into proximity to each other; or perhaps more exactly, it is to put the user into a position to establish such links by moving such materials into closer proximity to the user.

Why are such links important? Because all understanding, all knowledge necessarily entails context. On the nonmystical plane, there is no unitary reality. A thing is understandable, knowable, only in relation to another thing. We are now entering an era of revolutionary change precisely because information technology is providing us with new methods of linking objects that exist in widely dispersed environments—the ability to establish radically new contexts.

If a collection is a set of linked objects, then how should we conceive of an object? Let us, for our purposes here, view an object as a *text* in the broadest sense—i.e., a closed set of signs or symbols that have meaning to any user who has the ability to decode them. In the traditional environment, the user normally brings the code (e.g., the natural language) to the text. We must, in any case, take care to distinguish the code from the context, for both are fundamental prerequisites for understanding. The context is rather a relationship among texts. We should also recognize, moreover, that every document consists of a multiplicity of contexts—its constituent parts—which is to say a multiplicity of texts.

Using this definition, then, a document is, to be sure, an object—but we must also admit that a part of a document can be an object as well. In fact, several parts of a document can be an object. Several parts of several documents can together constitute an object. Several documents can be an object. Every collection, then, is in effect an object—and most objects can be viewed as collections of objects. The significance of this phenomenon—let us call it for our purposes *object embedment*—for the future of information services should not be underestimated. We have always understood object embedment in the abstract—but information technology is providing us with the ability to work with it in reality. It is perhaps related to the concept of "granularity." There are, for example, large-grained and small-grained databases. A large-grained database is presumably one which, using our definitions, contains objects that themselves contain objects, and so forth. In a way, therefore, the traditional library collection is a kind of large-grained object—or even a kind of large-grained document, which has been written or authored by bibliographers. One can read that document—or parts of that document, or the surrogates of that document—in a catalog. It is for this reason that finding and reading and thinking—and even writing—are really all variations of a single activity: context building, the creation of collections of objects. It is this object creation and manipulation—which is to say this collection development and management (done, to the extent possible, directly by the user)—which must form the basis of any future information services.

The Three Tiers

In the library we have traditionally distinguished among three collection tiers. See figure 1.

The upper tier is the universe of publication—all of the documents to which someone could gain access, with an adequate investment of time. This universe is, of course, a mess—in the sense that it is fundamentally uncontrolled; while parts of it are, to be sure, subject to some bibliographical control, those instances of control are not coordinated, so that this universe ultimately lacks any real system. A second collection tier is the personal collection, i.e., all objects used by a particular user to do a particular kind of work at a particular time. The objects that comprise the personal collection may derive from many sources, exist in different formats, and be the property of various owners. This collection tier is constantly changing, as the work and perspectives of the individual user change.

In order to facilitate the creation of the personal collection from the universe of publication, the library creates an intermediate set of documents, the local collection, that serves as a representation of the universe of publication. This intermediate set is very carefully selected and controlled to meet the perceived and projected needs of local users; its purpose is to function in part as a substitute for the universe of publication, which is not effectively or easily accessible because of its uncontrolled, chaotic nature.

When we speak of disintermediation in the context of collection services, therefore, we mean the reduction—gradually over time—of the significance of the intermediate set for the purposes of the local user. Our aim must be—when the technology and the culture permit—to apply some of the resources that we now use to select and control the intermediate set to the increased control of the universe of publication. If all research libraries could engage cooperatively in this effort, then perhaps our combined resources could provide a substantial segment of the universe of publication with sufficient organization and transparency that our users could draw directly on that universe for the creation of their personal collections, rather than being obliged to work always through the mediating agency of the intermediate set. Why should we want to do this in the long term? Because there are aspects of the intermediate

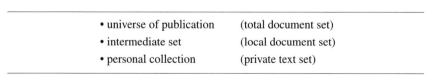

* universe of publication   (total document set)
* intermediate set   (local document set)
* personal collection   (private text set)

Figure 1. Traditional Collection Tiers

set, as a mediation service, that are—without question—intrusive. Our goal must be, therefore, a condition in which the user, as much as possible, makes his or her own selection decisions. It is admittedly difficult to say at this time whether that will ever be possible, but our hope must be that technology and bibliographical organization will allow us eventually to empower the user by reducing the level of mediation.

Organization

Our traditional organization in libraries is divided into a subjective and an objective service orientation. See figure 2.

The objective side of the operation views the needs of the user community as a given and tries to add value to specific information objects in order to increase the capacity of such objects to meet those local information needs. The subjective side takes the objective collection—intermediate set, universe of publication—as a given and works with local users to increase their capacity to make use of available objects to meet their evolving information needs. The weakness of the subjective side is the potentially inadequate understanding about how objects relate to each other and how their relations change over time; the liability on the objective side is the failure to understand in sufficient depth the continuously evolving needs of the user community. On the objec-

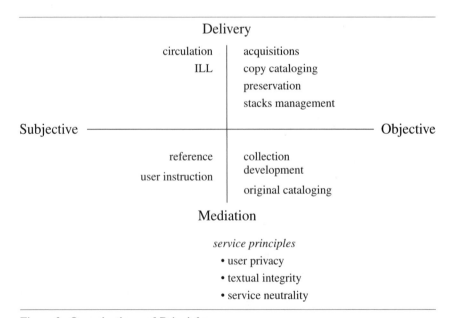

Figure 2. Organization and Principles

tive side, the focus is always on potential utility, while on the subjective side the emphasis is usually on actual use. The objective orientation tends therefore to be the more abstract and the subjective orientation the more practical.

At the same time, library operations can and should be viewed increasingly as falling into two main categories, which I have written about often before: delivery and mediation.[1] Mediation services are focused on content and are mainly concerned with the distinctions between individual information objects. Delivery services, on the other hand, are the more technical, engine-like side of the operation. This technical aspect is an essential component of library operations—and has been since Alexandria; it did not suddenly evolve with the advent of computer technology. Delivery services form the machine that keeps the operation running. (Information technology, library systems, should be understood as also belonging in general to the delivery side of the operation.) It focuses more on form, on the naming of objects rather than their distinguishing relationships, and does not easily brook differences. Perhaps the strongest inclination of delivery services is, in fact, to treat every object as much (as possible) the same, because differences impair efficiency—and the purpose of delivery services is to strive continuously to create a more efficient operating process.

Mediation services have more prestige—it is there that we employ most of our professionals (although that is also slowly changing)—but delivery services have ultimately the higher priority, because without effective delivery services the library cannot function, regardless of the level of mediation it provides. (If the engine does not run—if you don't pay your bills, if receipts go unprocessed, if materials do not get back on the shelf, if books cannot circulate—then the library is effectively out of business.) Most of the real crises in library operations happen in delivery. When they happen, libraries routinely—sometimes blatantly, sometimes covertly—shift resources, temporarily or permanently, from mediation into delivery.

We have traditionally organized operations in the library on the basis of the service sequence: (a) the object is selected, (b) it is acquired and processed, (c) it is presented to the user, and (d) the user is assisted in its location and use. Then, if all goes as it should, the experience from that work directly with the user informs the selection of new material—thus completing the circuit. Operations that are adjacent in that sequence are, therefore, often and quite reasonably linked in the organizational structure. We consequently have tried to connect acquisitions and cataloging as closely as we can, as we have circulation and reference.

Linking operations across the vertical and horizontal divisions (in figure 2) is probably the primary organizational challenge for library management. The division between the subjective and objective sides of mediation is often, in my experience, less contentious; the purpose of both sides is, in a way, to help people think, so that the private and relatively informal nature of those operations reduces the level of friction between the subjective and objective sides. In delivery services, on the other hand, if the subjective and objective sides get "out of synch," the gnashing of gears throughout the library system can be deafening—because these are two technical components of the same engine. If they do not run in unison, one will inevitably interrupt or destabilize the other.

A range of fundamental service principles derives from these operations. Let us select three more obvious examples. From the subjective side, one of the most obvious principles is user privacy. The library must protect the user's right to free and open access without the knowledge or interaction of other users. The objective equivalent is perhaps textual integrity. The library is expected to protect the original composition of the text from any intrusion, so that the text is, as much as possible, exactly as the writer intended. The subjective side aims to protect the reader, while the objective side is concerned also with the rights of the author. Both the subjective and the objective combine in the third fundamental principle, service neutrality. The library must avoid entering too obtrusively into the information process, lest it influence or skew the judgment or decisions of its users. This third principle is the source of much of the confusion and soul-searching that pervades the library profession—because most librarians do believe unreservedly in this fundamental principle, while at the same time spending most of their working day refuting it in practice—constantly steering the user to one source rather than another, in effect guiding (if not actually participating in the making of) user decisions at every level.

As we move increasingly into an online environment, we must consider how this organizational structure should evolve. If we succeed in our quest for disintermediation (which is, of course, nothing other than an effort to fulfill more effectively the principle of service neutrality), how should this structure change? In order to answer this question, we must give some thought to the nature of research.

The Research Process

In considering the research process in the abstract, we must begin with the notion of "primacy," by which I mean the designation of a particular text upon which the research will focus. This text serves as the core of the personal collection. Once primacy is defined, all other texts become potential contexts, although obviously only a subset of those other texts finally plays that role. See figure 3.

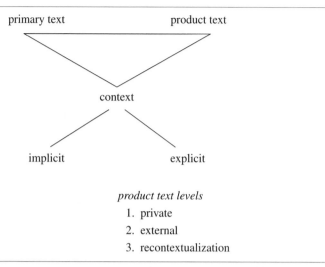

primary text   product text

context

implicit   explicit

product text levels
1. private
2. external
3. recontextualization

Figure 3. Research Components

While it is clear that scholars in humanities disciplines concentrate their work on primary texts, what about the scholars of the natural and social sciences, whose focus is on nature and society rather than primarily on texts? Let us posit tentatively that those disciplines do in fact focus on texts—that the primary focus of such scholars is in fact not on the natural or social worlds, but rather always on the core literature, which (in)forms their understanding of the natural or social world. Such scholars are therefore (let us say) always working first with a set of information objects, and only secondarily (through the medium of those objects) with the natural and social world. There is, therefore, no difference between the term "primary literature" in the sciences and in the humanities. The central activity in all cases is work with the information object.

The primary text is analyzed, understood, made to mean, on the basis of its relationship with other texts, i.e., through context. We can therefore stipulate two broad categories of context. Implicit context provides background for the work with the primary text, while explicit context is that text (those other writings) which refers specifically to the primary text. We also should note that the availability or existence of a library is not necessary for this model to function: this abstract process is taking place all the time. All analysis focuses on some kind of primary text, which can be understood only by virtue of a context. The function of the library is always precisely to increase or boost the extent and capacity of the context so that understanding can be enhanced.

In every act of research—or textual understanding—the researcher necessarily creates a *product text*. We can distinguish at least three levels of such product texts. The first is the private level, in the sense that anyone reading anything necessarily creates a mental text, separate from the text read; but that product text is entirely private—the personal product (text) of understanding. At a second level, the researcher may externalize that product text—i.e., pass it on in some form to other people. The third product text level is an expansion of the second, in which the product text becomes a formal part of the explicit context, to be taken into account in any future analysis of the primary text.

No one legitimately enters an academic library except to create a level two or level three product text. One can enter a public library with the intention of creating a level one product text (although many people also use public libraries for level two or three), but to enter an academic library to create a level one product text is to be a nonproductive consumer—someone who draws from but fails to replenish the total store of knowledge. One is expected to use an academic library either to create term papers or reports, or to write tests or lectures (level two), or to create articles, books, or databases that will ultimately be published and form part of the new context (level three).

This simple model can be applied, of course, to all forms of intellectual work—including all library operations. Cataloging, for example, views the item in hand as the primary text and, on the basis of classification tools (implicit context) and knowledge about the subject (explicit context), creates a product text in the form of the catalog record. (Collection development perhaps views the universe of publication as its primary text and the local collection as a product text.) The central mission of information services is always to ensure that this cycle of knowledge production continues to operate effectively. How does the library do this and how should it proceed with that work in the future age of transition? The answer is to be found in two fundamental library functions: archiving and metadata.

Archiving and Metadata

The first of these functions is archiving. For some information service experts, this is an exceedingly dull activity. Few rewards and little money will probably derive from large scale archiving—which is why the rest of the information services community is expecting libraries to take care of it. And we will. Some aspects of archiving, to be sure, have received much attention. One of the more prominent is certainly "backwards compatibility"—the capacity to access information originally created with now obsolete hardware and software. This will require an ongoing program of "refreshing" or migration as part of a national archiving process. One imagines that all electronic information ultimately will be in a more or less continuous state of being copied—not only to ensure its longevity, but also to make certain that it is upgraded, so that it remains accessible by way of contemporary technology.

The belief that libraries should assume responsibility for the future of archiving is, of course, not shared by everyone. See, for example, Brewster Kahle's current effort to archive large segments of the content of the World Wide Web.[2] Certainly he is of the opinion that there will be a market for such long-term historical content. However, one wonders—perhaps somewhat naively—whether such automatic and total archiving will eventually bring us to a point at which, by virtue of the finitude of natural language vocabulary, any search, regardless of what filter is used, will still result in too much information to be useful for any purpose (except perhaps counting hits); again, if the function of information services is to reduce the amount of time required by the user to locate needed information, will not the indiscriminate archiving of all Web content ultimately undermine that fundamental objective? Not only do we need, therefore, to create more effective selection mechanisms for what is archived, but we must also consider any options available to increase or augment the facility of natural language for purposes of searching and retrieval.

This whole problem of archiving is, of course, merely one of the latest manifestations of the eternal dilemma of preservation. On the one hand, one goal of preservation always must be to protect the future from the present. The present is exceedingly selfish and is fully prepared to expend all of its resources in satisfying its own needs. Some authority must intervene, therefore, to ensure that some of those resources are diverted to meet the needs of the future—so that the future will have at least some of the information it will require. At the same time, however, preservation also must be prepared to protect the present from the past, because the sheer weight of the past can immobilize the present. We are moving now into an era in which very significant portions of our present resources must be diverted to retaining past information—so that the cost of maintaining what we already have is beginning to impair our ability to acquire new materials, to continue to grow. One of the biggest questions today confronting preservation, and information services at large, is what price history? One of the most serious challenges we face is to create systems to help us decide (to put it bluntly) what to lose, what to forget.

Preservation selection, however, is no longer simply a matter of deciding what gets preserved and what does not. The revolution in information services—especially that quality we have referred to as object embedment—does provide preservation selection with some expanded options. See figure 4.

All preservation selection must start with the identification of specific items as being of key significance. We must make certain that these are immediately accessible indefinitely and in their totality. At the same time, some materials, while deserving of maintenance in their entirety, may not be required for such

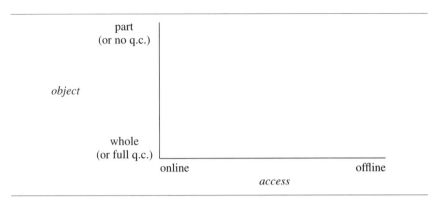

Figure 4. Archiving

immediate access—so that we can maintain them offline. Still others may need to be rapidly accessible, but may not need to be totally accurate—in the sense that we may not need to expend resources to ensure their total accuracy. This is admittedly a somewhat radical perspective—but ensuring totally accurate transmission over time can be expensive. In some cases we may want to pass only parts of larger objects on to the future or we may find that it is most cost effective not to invest the level of quality control that may be necessary to ensure 100 percent accuracy.

The other major responsibility or focus of information services in the future must be metadata. The term metadata—data about data—is an important one that the discipline of bibliography has greatly needed for some time. (The prefix "meta-" means next to, outside of, behind, related but separate.) The most important work done on metadata standards for online resources is certainly the Dublin Core. (I would recommend Warwick Cathro's summary as one good place for the less initiated to begin learning about this subject.[3])

The purpose of metadata is to facilitate the creation of object contexts. We can therefore divide metadata into two broad categories, nominal and relational. See figure 5.

I make this distinction partially because it also supports the organizational distinction between mediation and delivery. The delivery services operation is more concerned with nominal metadata, in that delivery services requires identifiers for all objects, but prefers to treat them as much the same as possible. Mediation services, on the other hand, is more focused on relational metadata, in that its aim is to distinguish and compare the content of information objects. We can further divide relational metadata into two broad categories. One is descriptive metadata, which can take at least two forms. There is discrete description, which identifies different qualities that are essentially equal

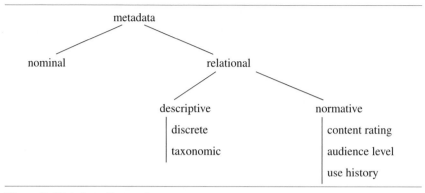

Figure 5. Metadata Categories

in value (e.g., formats, genres). There is also what we might label taxonomic metadata, which entails some hierarchical system of relationships—the most obvious example being controlled subject categories.

We also must distinguish a second kind of relational metadata—one to which we will need to devote increasing attention in the future—which we will designate as normative metadata. This is information that evaluates other information, mainly as a basis for information selection—for deciding what to read. One form of metadata must be content rating, which is roughly equivalent to editorial decision making, except that it is made subsequent to publication. This is a change in the publishing sequence that we must expect and welcome in the future. Rather than someone submitting something for publication, which editors then decide whether to publish, the writer can put something up on the network, in effect publishing it. Subsequent to that act of publication, scholars in the field can then determine the significance of that publication and can communicate that significance to others. (We are seeing now an early version of this process in the posting of pre-prints, the most notable example being the pre-print service for physics articles at Los Alamos.[4]) In the case of scholarly information, that responsibility should be delegated in the future to designated, trusted experts. The conclusions of those experts, the content rating, should take the form of metadata, which then can be used for searching.

Content rating is one of the metadata elements identified as part of the Warwick Framework, which is a suggested expansion of the Dublin Core. Carl Lagoze, in a report on the Warwick Framework,[5] lists, as one example of content rating, the Platform for Internet Content Selection,[6] which rates the suitability of different Web pages for access by children. As Carl Lagoze has noted, however, that same rating software could be used for any kind of rating—including presumably that done by experts in specialized scholarly disciplines.

Another form of normative metadata should be some indication of the target audience: for whom is this publication intended? What background must the reader have in order to understand the publication? Is the publication intended for the lay reader? For undergraduates? If intended for advanced readers, how much of the previous literature must be known in order to understand it? This relates also perhaps to a concept I have discussed previously, which I have called "concentric stratification."[7] The revolution in information services provides us with the opportunity and the necessity to develop less linear methods of graphic communication. Although information objects in the paper environment are of a totally linear construction (a codex is conceptually simply a folded scroll), writers do not write from front to back, nor do readers usually read that way (except for very short works, or certain kinds of material like belles lettres). We need therefore more realistic and effective methods of writing and reading in the online environment. A (virtual) stack of increasingly larger discs is one model. On the smallest, top stratum is the citation or, possibly, an abstract. The next disc contains that same information, further expanded to include the most significant points in the writing. The next stratum contains that same information, plus further, more detailed and enhanced information—and so forth.

If some kind of nonlinear approach like concentric stratification were to evolve, standards could be created for specific strata in any scholarly publication. One aspect of such standardization would be to define different strata for different audiences. A reader would know which stratum of a particular publication to enter and read, depending upon how acquainted the reader assumes herself to be with the topic. The object itself, moreover, then becomes a kind of teaching or learning mechanism, in that the reader can teach herself by reading vertically—i.e., one stratum at a time. Each stratum thus provides a context for the stratum preceding it—and the most significant information is repeated and is developed through each stratum.

While the reader or editor is responsible for content rating, and while the writer is primarily responsible for the definition of audience level, there is also a third category of normative metadata that can be generated more automatically and can be used to supplement the first two: use history. We should be able to capture and make public what specific groups of users are reading. This will require that we begin as soon as possible to "catalog" users into categories. In order to decide what to read, the user could take into account what other categories of users are reading. What are other scholars in the field reading? What are undergraduates reading? What are experts in discipline A reading in discipline B? Or what are they not reading in discipline B, so that I, an expert in discipline A, can see what my colleagues are overlooking?

We also should bear in mind that the author can achieve a result somewhat similar to normative metadata by making a more extended or creative use of tagging within the document. Certainly the writer can link to other information beyond the publication—that is the future of hypertext citation. But if some new mode of writing like concentric stratification proves not to be an option, the author still can engage in a kind of internal linking to add new dimensions to the reading experience. Tagging should be learned and used, therefore, as part of the writing process—and it may be that such tagging will eventually provide us with some opportunity to increase the capacity of natural language to permit more effective archiving and retrieval. If vertical reading and writing, which allow the "core" of the document to be repeated and developed, are not a possibility, the writer at least can link parts of the publication internally. Different parts of the publication could be connected to other parts. Or, to approach the same problem slightly differently, tagging could be used by the writer to differentiate or define the significance of different parts of the publication—a kind of internal content rating.

We began by expressing a hope that the next generation of computers would have the capacity to do some of the reading for the reader. It now becomes clear that we have, in a way, always had that capacity—we have always provided that service—it has always been the fundamental purpose of information services or bibliography or cataloging. It is the service that provides the reader-user with the capacity to create new contexts. Our goal now must be to enhance that service by exploiting advances in information technology.

Assuming the service structure posited earlier, based on the division between delivery and mediation, we can now conclude that delivery services should focus increasingly on archiving, while mediation services should concentrate more on the fast expanding area of the creation and use of metadata. We also must aim, however, to use this increased emphasis on archiving and metadata to bring about a greater administrative and cultural synthesis between delivery and mediation services for library management purposes. We must close the gap between these two cultures, because archiving and metadata will be fully effective only to the extent that they are mutually supporting. Backwards compatibility, to take one example that we have already mentioned, is not simply a delivery/archiving problem. It does not simply entail the ability to regenerate a set of signs that were originally produced by a now obsolete hardware/software configuration. Backwards compatibility also must ensure the ability of readers to understand those signs. That understanding derives from codes and contexts—so that we must concentrate (as we always have in collection development) not on the archiving of documents but rather on the creation and maintenance of collections. Some fundamental concepts of collection development, therefore, come in a way to their fruition in the activity of long-term archiving—although the collection developer likely will play a very different role in that future archiving work.

Beyond Documentation

Is, finally, the provision of access to the universe of publication enough? Is it possible to expand the concept of library services even beyond that universe (without colliding with the mystical plane)? If so, the answer is perhaps to be found in the previously mentioned concept of "primacy." I took the position earlier that all science and social science research, like the humanities, ultimately starts from a text written by someone else—a set of information objects. But perhaps that is too narrow a perspective. Robert Losee has recently argued that information science needs to expand its scope beyond information objects produced by human beings—to include the study of all information production and transfer, including signals of nonhuman origin.[8] For more assistance along this line, we can reach back twenty years, and resuscitate yet again the many faceted concept of "textuality." In a classic article published in 1976, Frederic Jameson defined textuality as "a methodological hypothesis whereby the objects of study of the human sciences (but not only the human ones: witness the genetic 'code' of DNA!) are considered to constitute so many texts which we *decipher* and *interpret,* as distinguished from the older views of those objects as realities or existants or substances which we in one way or another attempt to *know*."[9] The world is, therefore, ultimately a text, which one interprets rather than knows—in the same way perhaps that one never attains the direct knowledge of the nonmystical plane, but rather only deciphers or interprets by way of mediation and context.

Perhaps we can expand the concept of information services, therefore, finally beyond the traditional library and into all research of the natural and social worlds. The real purpose of information services thus is to provide the context for understanding all perceived objects—not just information objects in the traditional sense, but all objects from which learning can be derived. Only through such an expansion of information services can we hope to achieve the long sought functional coalescence of the library, the laboratory, and the classroom.

Conclusion

To summarize, disintermediation should be a goal for all information services. We should aim to connect the user more directly to the universe of publication whenever possible. This can be accomplished only by significantly improving delivery and mediation services—or specifically by providing more effective archiving constructs and more incisive metadata, including especially normative metadata. That normative metadata, however, should not have its origins in the mediator (i.e., in the library)—but should rather be supplied by the reading experts (content rating), by the writer (e.g., defining audience level), and automatically (by, e.g., use history). We also have said that we must try to integrate information services into the broader research activity at large. Such changes will be wrenching for ourselves and our users, but to overturn long held, cherished principles is a quality of revolution.

Returning to our fundamental service principles (figure 2), we can see now that privacy will need to be compromised somewhat, if we are to apply the history of use as a basis for searching and evaluation. Textual integrity will not survive object embedment, nor should it. We must be prepared to compromise here, as well—and to accept that the integrity of some texts may be unavoidably violated. Service neutrality has always been a charade and a source of acute emotional tension in library services—mainly because we enter so deliberately and intrusively into the research process, while at the same time self-righteously disparaging such intrusion. If we can reduce that intrusion somewhat, especially through such agencies as normative bibliography, then we can more easily acknowledge such guidance as one of the library's truly core functions.

On the other hand, we must also realize, however, that privacy, textual integrity, and service neutrality are, on the whole, only surface values. There are, at the same time, more fundamental values—an underlying ideology—that we must take every precaution not to deny or abandon. Indeed, the more we move into the online environment, the more essential it is that we remain strong advocates of that ideology. For that reason, any truly effective redefinition of the traditional service paradigm must include a very real and visible political action component.

The commercial information business is growing rapidly—and we live in an age that is fascinated by business to a point of obsession. Business is contemporary society's highest ideal. Our understanding of management in general is defined for us by business. We read books written by business managers for business managers and we try to apply those same methods and principles to our own work. We make the mistake above all of assuming that we are in the service business—but this cannot be the case, because our primary purpose is service. The primary purpose of the service business, on the other hand, is not service, but business. It is revenue generation—not the use of funding to increase access, but the use of access to increase revenue. This is an ideology that is fundamentally antithetical to our own and, if that ideology is allowed to grow unchecked, it will ultimately impair and degrade access to some kinds of information—most notably the specialized scholarly variety.

The most significant threat to access on the horizon is therefore without question the galloping commercialization of information. It is the capacity provided by information technology for publishers to limit radically access to the information under their control. Anyone who imagines we are entering an era of increased access is destined to be greatly disappointed. There is, in fact, a good chance we are entering an era of effectively reduced access to information as compared to the traditional paper era—because information technology provides the proprietors of information with a much greater capacity to reduce access. Some publishers will no doubt use that capacity to make needed information scarce, in order to drive up its value and price. Anyone who thinks this will not happen is blind to what has been going on in the paper environment. Small libraries especially may be operating on the assumption that they are entering a new and better era, in which they will finally be able to provide remote access for their users to all kinds of information they do not own. That probably will not happen. If current trends continue, there is a very good chance that smaller libraries will have inadequate access in the future, for the same reason they have inadequate access in the present—they do not have enough money. For that is what will be required for access in the future—a great deal of money. Unlike the present, there will be no alternative avenue of access in the future. If things continue to proceed in their present direction, there will be no equivalent of interlibrary loan in an online environment. Libraries will either pay what publishers demand for access or they will not have such access.

Everything I have said in this chapter—and much of what was said at the conference—is just so much self-indulgent fantasy and wishful thinking if the current relationships of information ownership and production remain in place. Some of those relationships will have to be overturned if information services are to move forward. A new service paradigm cannot possibly be achieved, in other words, without the decommercialization of significant parts of the publication process, without the disintermediation of the traditional methods of specialized scholarly publishing *per se,* and without the reappropriation of at least some of the responsibility for scholarly information exchange by the academy itself.

That can be achieved in only two ways. First, we must develop concepts—methods, theories, experiments, testbeds—that will provide practicable alternatives to the current methods of information exchange (practicable in the sense that they will provide writers with the same rewards, and they will provide readers with equivalent or superior methods of access and control, as is the case in the traditional environment). Second, we must use direct action—

which is to say that we must galvanize our college and university administrations. We must explain exactly what is going on and why it is that we may end up spending more and more money to provide access to less and less information. We must work above all with the faculty, to help them learn how they can use other, more effective methods to exchange information than relying on traditional publishers. We must help faculty to understand the fact that if we continue to exchange information in the traditional manner, it will lead ultimately to a severe degradation of scholarly information exchange and possibly of scholarship itself.

This revolution upon which we are embarking, therefore, is not simply technical or bibliographic—but is rather, like all real revolutions, fundamentally political. Its realization will require political skills and commitment. It will require a clarity of vision, an assertiveness, an audacity—and, above all, courage—for these are career-threatening issues that we raise in a career-threatening time.

We are now rapidly approaching a point at which we as a profession will need to make a choice. Either we step back—admitting, in effect, that these are not our affairs—but that these issues of access and commercialization must rather be the concerns of the producers and the proprietors of information, that we are only the mediators, the public servants, the helpers. Or we stand up and accept the moral responsibility that is being offered to us at this very special time in the history of libraries and scholarship. For those of us who, at this time at the end of the twentieth century, are still proud to call ourselves librarians, the right choice is clear—and there is no doubt in my mind that we will ultimately make it.

Notes

1. Ross Atkinson, "Access, Ownership, and the Future of Collection Development," in *Collection Management and Development: Issues in an Electronic Era,* ed. Peggy Johnson and Bonnie MacEwan (Chicago: American Library Association, 1994), 94–96.
2. "The Internet Archive," http://www.archive.org.
3. "Metadata: An Overview," http://www.nla.gov.au/nla/staffpaper/cathro3.html.
4. "e-Print archive," http://xxx.lanl.gov.
5. Carl Lagoze, "The Warwick Framework: A Container Architecture for Diverse Sets of Metadata," *D-Lib Magazine* (July/August 1996), http://www.dlib.org/july96/lagoze/07lagoze.html.
6. "Platform for Content Internet Selection," http://www.w3.org/PICS/.
7. Ross Atkinson, "Networks, Hypertext, and Academic Information Services: Some Longer-Range Implications," *College & Research Libraries* 54 (May 1993): 208.
8. Robert M. Losee, "A Discipline Independent Definition of Information," *Journal of the American Society for Information Science* 48 (March 1997): 254–69.
9. Frederic Jameson, "The Ideology of the Text," *Salmagundi* 31/32 (1975/76): 205.

2

Seamless Information Environments and Seamless Management Structures: Where Are Our Aspirations Leading Us?

Eugene L. Wiemers

For the last several years, library managers have had the opportunity to live and work through the early stages of providing information support to the next generation of scholars. A prominent metaphor of the design of library services is the creation of "seamless" information environments. Widely used in the information technology literature, the concept of a seamless environment serves as an ideal for individual libraries,[1] for database services offered by libraries,[2] and for library consortia.[3] This metaphor implies a very broad vision of what scholars will be able to do—find and use all information content, in all formats that support their scholarship, presented in ways they can easily connect. Saying this drives planning. Making it happen drives librarians crazy. The user now wants:

to find bibliographic information that leads to both primary and secondary sources;

to get access to data (citations, primary and secondary sources) with tools appropriate to the source, download or copy the data from print or electronic sources, and put the data in a form they can later store and manage;

to manipulate data with bibliographic, statistical, word processing, or graphics support programs; store it in databases; and achieve instant recall;

to incorporate the results of the analysis in written documentation using word processing and graphics;

to print the results to paper or files, to put it out in HTML or other standard languages for others to see and use.

And users want to be able to think while they are doing all this. The users I know and observe do not think of these as separate processes. They think of them as parts of one process that often occur more-or-less simultaneously in the library. Increasingly, users do not expect to encounter a bureaucratic structure that assigns different staff to different steps of the research process or a system that requires them to go to different places to do parts of their work. Users already see the seamlessness librarians and technologists have created and they want it to work for them now.

The library staff often finds itself in the position of having to answer questions for all the steps. This happens because libraries have service points staffed with smart people who have a professional ethic of service and knowledge of the information content. Users seem to expect a staff who can help with content, who can help users understand the information, and who can get information into forms they can use. Libraries may not like the combination, but users' expectations derive in part from the users' sense that information content is what drives the selection, acquisition, and presentation of the material, and the users' belief that staff who help them find information can also help them use it. This expectation of one-stop service falls directly from the aspiration of seamless and user-friendly access to information and, though the implications are unexpected, librarians will embrace the implications as they have embraced the vision.

Seamless Information Environments

For the past several years I have been working in a management position in an environment where responsibility for information content, responsibility for information delivery systems, and responsibility for instructional and user services for both information and information management tools for a college campus are centralized in a collaborative management team. For the past year, I also have been working with colleagues at two other colleges to build a consortial effort that links both library and computing services in efforts to build joint or collaborative information services. This is very interesting and very complex work, in both the organizational and technical senses. I do not think of this experience as something new. I think of it as collection management and public services.

I think of it as collection management because it starts from the question "What does the user need?" and because it requires outreach, liaison programs, and systematic feedback about users' needs. Tony Ferguson, in previous collection management institutes and in direct response to the lament that the collection officer or bibliographer is dying as a professional category, reminds us that the essential skill that will secure the future of the collections librarian is that he or she has the tools to learn and to meet what the users need.[4]

This should be a given as the starting premise. Many information technologists start with a different question: "What could the user do?" This question leads to many interesting new technologies and techniques, but as a management principle for an information service organization, it is flawed. Focusing only on the latest thing, the new software, or the new book, for that matter, will inevitably lead to spending time on things that are not needed. Attention to the latest thing sometimes focuses on innovations scholars find positively irritating. The logical extension of the application of the question "What could users do?" as a starting point for service development is the practice of the software giant that puts out new releases of software addressing problems users have not encountered by adding functions users never dreamed of. These so-called upgrades force users to abandon tools that work and spend money they do not want to spend in order to get functionality that does not address their real problems. The instinct that builds on the model of the librarian as collection builder should start by asking what users need and work out from there. This is one of the basic insights of librarianship—ask what the user needs.

I also think of managing an electronic information environment as public service. The skills of assessing user needs also are tempered by the insight of the reference interview—the insight that people do not often say what they need, so it is a service provider's job to find out what they mean. About a year ago, I got a phone call from a local resident who was unclear about whether our library was open to the public and what services she was able to use. She said she was "doing a research paper on a computer program," and could she use the computers in the library to continue her work while she was in town? I asked what program she was working on and she said it was Microsoft Word. So I asked what version of Word, to make sure we had what she needed. Well, it turns out no particular version would be needed, because what she really wanted to do was to print her thesis out on one of the "free" printers located in the library so it would be ready at the end of her vacation for presentation at Yale, where she was completing her degree. She was writing a research paper "in" Microsoft Word, not "on" it.

The key skills of collection management and public service are to try starting from what users need, and to know that they do not always say what they need. With these skills, we build a system of information support. We start from the users' needs in the selection of materials in print, materials in electronic form, and in the interfaces we choose. It is a system that includes people to help, people to train, books and journals to read, systems to search, and databases to probe. The information needs of the user drive the content of the system. This premise seems obvious, but information service providers often forget its importance.

Users do not want a system or a structure. They want the information. What we have begun to give them, in our attempt to build a seamless information environment, however, is a system or a structure based on demand. Eventually we may be positioned to provide a virtual library that resembles a research library in which the content represents a model or microcosm of the store of recorded knowledge. Right now we are in an era where the content base of what we make available electronically is not intended to represent a sample of all available information. Rather the content of electronic information is driven by the demands of users. So information services managers pay attention to what users ask for, but they also have to pay attention to what is used. Almost all librarians work in institutions with the technical capacity to make virtually any item available electronically. The critical questions are "How many?" "Of what?" and "How accessible should they be?" The legal obstacles are vexing, but the economic obstacles still force us to choose which items or which information products will receive the premier treatment of universal access, day and night, by our users. These choices are made on the basis of user demand or perceived user need. In a research library, for both print and electronic resources, demand is not the only consideration, for, if it were, there would be little support for small academic programs. But for electronic resources, more strongly than for others, demand is still the primary consideration, as no research institution is yet able to provide universal twenty-four-hour access to large bodies of material that it expects, on the average, to be used only rarely. So in today's environment, demand drives content.

If demand drives content, how should information systems work? My own experience and my faith in the future of librarianship is that content drives design, both in how individual products are put together and in how we build systems to bring them to users. Paul Evan Peters used to talk about the Almost Good Enough to Use test.[5] This is the threshold condition in which scholars' assessment of an information product or support system is that it is almost something that might meet a real need in their research or teaching. These are the products to which librarians should start to pay attention. All of us have had the experience of looking at a new electronic product or gadget that is full of attributes one of my colleagues calls "whiffiness." The high-end sound systems, the "whiffy" graphics presentations, and super fast speeds that are optimized for games are features that attract twelve-year-olds and sell hardware. What makes an electronic research environment different from a twelve-year-old's game room is that the design has to serve an end—an end that is determined, and not just conditioned, by content. The test is "Does the technology make the content accessible in a way that serves the need?"

Some of the new toys are almost good enough to use and, when they are, information services and library managers need to pay attention and plan for them. In the past year or so, many of us have learned the value of reduced, though tasteful, graphics in the design of Web pages because they make the systems feel more nimble. Choosing which kind of desktop hardware will be needed and how often it must be upgraded, based on the anticipated conditions in the software and database industry, has replaced the administrative practice of limiting information content based on the capabilities of the equipment we happen to have at the moment. Frequently changing where to get a particular database, based on both cost and ease of use, is another example of a practice to serve the research process at lower cost or greater ease, without reducing user choices. The design of an information support system for an academic institution, including desktops, networks, and services, must now be based on what information products you expect users to use, what their requirements are, and how often each product is expected to be used. This is what I mean by "content drives design."

So what do I think users need? They need a virtual library that is not a part of a network or a part of the library. It is the library and it is everywhere the user is. The library has a front door that is open twenty-four hours and users need as much information in it as we can afford to give them, presented as simply as we can make it. Users need the access tools, the productivity tools, and the research tools to find, manipulate, transfer, and disseminate the knowledge they produce. They need tools that help them transfer that knowledge to students and to other researchers. And they need help. They do not just think of the content of the system as the library. They think of the whole system as the library. They think it is a seamless environment and they expect us to make it that way.

Organizing Seamless Management Environments

When I think about managing the system I have just described, I know it does not sound simple. A very large body of literature and a goodly slice of popular culture centers on the management, or nonmanagement, of information industries and environments. Think of Dilbert, cubicles, teams, and bosses with pointy heads. I get such barbs aimed at me, and much of the implied ridicule is deserved. The management challenge is to find a way to make it look as if there are no boundaries between the information content and the information system and among information systems, and to make it look as if there are no institutional obstacles that impede users' movement through the content, tools, networks, and output devices that are essential to their scholarly work.[6] The questions are common in academic and research institutions. Should the library be joined with computing? Should there be a Chief Information Officer? If so, should it be a librarian, a technologist, or a scholar? Should the library be in charge? Or, in some contexts, should the library sully its good reputation as a service organization by trying to deliver computing service? Or, in other contexts, can the library that is still mired in the world of printed texts take on the skyrocketing service demands of a high technology field? Who in their right mind would think that an environment like this is possible to manage, anyway?

These questions translate into the language of turf, the language of conflict, and metaphors of smokestacks and boundaries. Rather than analyze the distribution of responsibilities for virtual library services or how they should be organized, I want to raise two images and reflect on why I do not think structure matters in the management of a virtual library.

Some years ago, I wandered into a library on a campus where the library is known for its instructional, outreach, and high quality user services. On the main floor, I saw a reference librarian quietly reading book reviews at a reference desk and I saw no users. There were computers surrounding the desk, an array of multi- and single-purpose workstations, and printed admonitions on each machine that they are *not for e-mail.* I then walked downstairs to a space apparently separate though in the same building, and obviously managed by a separate campus organization, which was full of computers. There were dozens of people talking to each other, working together on workstations, accessing databases, surfing the Internet, writing papers, and checking their e-mail.

The users in the so-called "computer lab" had full access to everything on the campus-wide network that was accessible to users in the "library" upstairs. They did not have access to the single-purpose databases, they did not have access to print collections, and they did not have any help. The "library" had everything the students needed to write better papers and do better projects, but they did not have the students. Nor did the students in the "computer lab" have any cues or staff to remind them that the collections of the library have materials that are not "on the Internet." In this particular setting, the users were forced to draw a line between the library and the computer center, and the library had drawn a line between its collections and the other services it was capable of providing in such a way that the users simply went elsewhere.

I do not know, but I can imagine, the management gulf that created this scene. There are classic management instincts to define mission and priorities in ways that maximize the visibility and importance of the manager. There are impulses that give credit and honor and glory to successes within a defined sphere and that seek to push away, or exclude, those things that threaten boundaries or dilute the track record of the manager. These are the forces that build smokestacks, carve out turf, and draw lines. The most recent expression of this phenomenon in my thinking has been to try to understand the distinction we have made between computers, libraries, and telephones. We often put, for very good reasons, our voice communications into a cost-recovery or even a profit center, but put our networks into the category of an essential or "free" service. So given the challenge of delivering a multichannel, multimedia video- and teleconferencing system to support both scholarly communication and the underlying information support that communication requires, do we have the management tools and structures in place to make it happen? Rather than build boundaries and define turf, library and information services managers need to pay attention to what Peter Drucker calls managers' first duty, "to subordinate their likes, wishes and preferences to the needs of the institution," and take the ego out of decision making.[7]

Users expect that the virtual library has no internal boundaries. Users will treat the virtual library as a seamless one, and the manager's job is to tear down smokestacks, erase lines, and identify and resolve conflicts in order to support the users' needs. Of course, organizations and missions are important, and, of course, two or more individuals can never truly be of one mind. The point of management, however, is to make the connections, bridge the gaps, resolve conflicts, and spread success around. This too may seem obvious, but a seamless electronic research environment is as oblivious of hierarchy as it is of boundary. This means that collaboration is the essential feature of management and that there is no room for self-aggrandizement. Unnecessary organizational obstacles eventually will result in a failure somewhere in the fabric that binds the library together. When it does, the user will not know or care whose fault it is.

In Vichy France, collaboration was not a nice word. In setting up a virtual library, collaboration and commitment to your partner's success are essential at all levels in information services and library organizations.[8] When the systems work, that is, when users find the information they need to support their work and get to use it in the ways they want to, it does not matter if they think the library did it or the computer center did it or the Internet did it. When the system works, it does not matter who is on top. The system will fail, however, if whoever is on top is not paying attention to the essential and essentially human connections that are needed to set up and maintain a seamless system.

Users also will expect they will be able to make the system look the way they want. All of us have been through the discussions with marketers on our library or institutional staffs who want the "environment" to "look and feel" a particular way. Some even want to restrict content to things consistent with the mission of the organization. In their model, "purpose" drives design or perhaps "image" drives design. I argue here that content should drive design and that a close connection between design and content improves the use of the system. For a scholarly information system, trying to use design as a form of control is futile, because users can design their own interfaces. With a few quick HTML keystrokes or by hiring a twelve-year-old designer, they can make the system look and feel the way they want. So even the credit that comes from organizing a good looking array of resources only goes so far as the first-level access tools. The researcher might like the graphics, but eventually users will design their own access tools and make them look the way they want, feel the way they want them to feel, and will use a design that makes products work better for them.

Having said all this, I come back to the role content plays in what we do. I do not mean by asserting the primacy of the role of content in the virtual library that "collection development" has primacy over "public services" in systems design. I mean that there is no way to draw the line between the two and that the user does not care. Our goal, as managers of these systems, should be to make sure that users get what they need in a way they can use it. Content also drives network design as well as the design of services that distribute and teach the use of productivity tools like word processors, spreadsheets, and databases. At least in academic or research environments, our work is to supply the content that supports scholarship, and systems should be optimized for scholarship and not for entertainment, public relations, or administrative functions.

Seamless Financial Structures

Are seamless financial structures possible in information or library services? Many of the presidents and treasurers with whom I have worked refer to them as "bottomless" financial structures rather than seamless. But just think a moment about where the library profession has come in terms of thinking about budgeting for information services. Start with the collection development or materials budget. Much of my professional career has been punctuated, though thankfully not preoccupied, with either building up or tearing down metaphors that attempt to draw the financial line between collections and services. Some will remember these attempts—"We use the materials budget for things we purchase or objects we own," then, "We do not have to own them, but they have to be things," then "They do not have to be things, but they have to replace things we once owned." Or "It certainly does not include applications software, only content," followed by "Applications software is OK, as long as it is required to get to particular content," and so on.

More recently, I have been involved directly in budgeting for desktop hardware, servers, and network infrastructure, which potentially leaves many more places to draw lines. This fall, many of us had the opportunity to turn on a new version of Lexis-Nexis that is everything we want our organizations to be—faster, cheaper, and better. It is not perfect, but it is a vast improvement over the old system for the ordinary scholar. But to prepare ourselves to accept this new tool, we had to budget for a campus-wide network that extends to the library in enough places that we could use a Web-based product as a production tool for reference. We had to make a commitment to teach people not only about Lexis-Nexis, but about the Web. We had to prepare the campus for a change that would put Web-based services as front-line production services for faculty and staff, a change that required new desktop equipment for about half the faculty and many of the staff, as well as a commitment to upgrade that equipment on a regular basis so it could keep up with the changes in Web browsers, graphics programs, memory, and speed that all come with Web-based services. And we had to build a network with sufficient bandwidth that we can promise to deliver services based on graphical interfaces without crashes and roadblocks. I will not estimate the total cost here for all these changes, but they had to be planned and budgeted. In addition to all the infrastructure, we had to hire all the people it takes to deliver the systems and teach people how to use them.

A library organization that is attempting to build a virtual electronic library cannot take this level of investment and this level of planning for granted. All this planning requires an institution-wide view of the infrastructure and human resources to make a digital environment real. Without the content, without the network, without the smart people who make it work, without the people in the library and information services organizations to teach people how to use it—without all of this, the library is a failure.

In many ways, the success of the institutions of learning and research we serve depends on our success in managing the transition to a virtual library. In this transition, there is very little room for narrow thinking. Discussions like the one outlined above about how to "protect" the acquisitions budget or similar discussions on how to "protect" the hardware budget are examples of "many pockets" budgeting that use budgets as tools to protect turf and draw lines. This approach works against the necessities of the information system as a whole and is as destructive in its effects as turf-building and line-drawing are in management of human resources. In the transition to a virtual library, budgeting is a tool to plan for and execute the steps and to account for the anticipated and unanticipated costs of building all the components of the system and the content it provides.

This is where the real work of collaboration becomes critical—in deciding who pays. I believe that each institution will find its own way to achieve the required level of financial collaboration within its own organizational culture. I will make two observations here. The first is that a model that expects the library to pay only for the information content, based on budgets built from the traditional assumptions about the costs of library materials, and expects computing organizations to pay for the rest, based on traditional assumptions about the role of computing as administrative or academic support, will not work for the virtual library. Too many inflexibilities are built into the current financial models, which have the effect of protecting the purchasing power for scholarly information and underestimating the dependence of that information on delivery systems, for the model to succeed in a digital world. Too many inflexibilities are also in the computing budgets, which relate to keeping up with industry trends regardless of user needs. The second observation is that such a model almost inevitably will mean that the "library" will get put in direct competition with the "computer center" in institutional resource allocation, when in fact they are highly dependent upon one another. The financial resources to build the virtual library need to be planned on an institution-wide basis and measured against the cost of not building the virtual library. Only with this broad perspective will it be possible to generate the resources that will make the virtual library work in the seamless way users expect.

Sacred cows, whether in the form of a protected serials budget or a protected hardware budget, will result in a distribution of resources that is less than optimal and may be destructive in the long run. As in managing the resources and the people, the role of erasing lines, connecting pieces of the project, making linkages, and collaborating effectively will make limited dollars go further and will end, based on the importance of the information systems to the success of the organization as a whole, with more resources rather than less.

One of the perverse results of our practice in research institutions of protecting the acquisitions budget, especially the serials budget, is not only to slow the rate of substitution of electronic for print resources, but also to reinforce the position of monopolists in the information-providing industry. We may be at a point where the role of monopolists in the software industry may drive us to similar models to protect software budgets. I am not willing, yet, to argue that it was or is wrong to strive for a differential price increase for serials compared to other parts of a research institution's budget, although it is getting exceedingly difficult to argue for a differential that places price increases for serials at five to ten times the rate of general price increases. I only observe here that the financial models we have advocated have inadvertently colluded to provide the financial support for monopoly power in the scholarly journals industry. I would hate to have this pattern extended to the software industry in general.

Conclusion

So where does this discussion leave us? The expertise that drives the virtual library comes from the collections librarians, the public service librarians, the catalogers, and information processing experts who listen to users, assess their needs, and pick good things that work, things that users want, and things that users will use. Collection development, public services, technical services, or information services staff face no threat in this world. There is no threat to libraries. This kind of library requires a commitment to the user and to the skills of continuously paying attention to needs of users that are greater than, more diverse than, and more rapidly changing than in either libraries or computing environments of the past.

In this environment, collection managers are managers. The work of collection builders is not directed just at faculty or other clientele, it is also necessarily directed to colleagues, technologists, and instructional staff, and it is different work than merely selecting a book or canceling a journal. I think that public services librarians always have thought managerially, in the sense that making connections and bridging gaps and connecting users with each other is part of the work. But public services librarians also will learn that their work will include knowing access tools, statistical packages and spreadsheets, and other productivity tools that users will have at their fingertips to turn information into knowledge. The managerial task of making connections also extends to technologists, who will design systems with particular products and services in mind, and to managers who will plan for changes in products based on the anticipated capabilities of the systems that support them. All of these are managerial acts that require high amounts of communication and high degrees of interdependence. The common professional requirement is commitment to users.

The key ingredients are expertise and collaboration. For the foreseeable future, our business as librarians will be to connect users to materials in multiple formats and to each other. At every level, reaching out, identifying user needs, and assembling and reassembling teams of people to get things done with a very broad vision of the user's needs will be essential to our success, because users already will see the seamlessness we seek. When things do not work, users say that "nothing is working." They do not seek a detailed diagnosis of where the break occurred and whose fault it was. We should not talk about "winners and losers" in the virtual library. If we see the world as winners and losers, we know who the loser really is. The user is the loser, and none of our institutions can afford to let that happen.

I know the transition to this broad a framework has been difficult for me. I was not aware of, let alone convinced, that issues such as bandwidth and desktop capacity were essential to the success of the library. I have had to learn, and keep learning, to trust my colleagues in order to make judgments today that will be vital to services two or three years from now. I am convinced that the broad vision of seamless service is the correct one and that, in this vision, the content and the librarians who provide it are not the center of the system, because there is no center. The system is a circle and the skills and professional commitments of this profession are essential parts of the circle.

Notes

1. Duke University, Fuqua School of Business home page: http://www.lib.duke.edu/fsb/index.htm (1 April 1998).
2. Massachusetts Library and Information Network, "Catalogs of Massachusetts Libraries," http://www.mlin.lkib.ma.us/catalogs.htm (1 April 1998).
3. Committee on Institutional Cooperation, CIC Center for Library Initiatives home page, 1997, http://nova.cic.uiuc.edu/CIC/cli/index.html# The Center for Library Initiatives (1 April 1998); Committee on Institutional Cooperation, "Overview: The CIC Virtual Electronic Library Project," 1998, http://ntx2.cso.uiuc.edu/cic/cli/velnew.html (1 April 1998).
4. Anthony W. Ferguson, "Collection Development Politics: The Art of the Possible," in *Collection Management and Development: Issues in an Electronic Era,* ed. Peggy Johnson and Bonnie MacEwan (Chicago: American Library Association, 1994), 29–41.
5. Paul Evan Peters, remarks at Oberlin Group annual meeting, Carleton College, Northfield, Minnesota (30 September 1994).
6. Peter V. Deekle and Ann DeKlerk, "Perceptions of Library Leadership in a Time of Change," *Journal of Library Administration* 17, no. 1 (1992): 55–75; Arthur P. Young, "Information Technology and Libraries: A Virtual Convergence," *Cause/Effect* 17, no. 3 (1994): 5–6, 12.
7. Robert P. Lenzer and Stephen S. Johnson, "Seeing Things As They Really Are," *Forbes* 159, no. 5 (1997): 122–28.
8. Richard Lynch, "Creating Partnerships: Forging a Chain of Service Quality," *Journal of Library Administration* 18, no. 1–2 (1993): 137–55.

3

Information Technologies and Educational Purposes: An Uneasy Alliance

John Howe

A number of years ago I spoke before a throng of librarians. I felt a bit of an impostor, speaking as a non-librarian to a gathering of professionals on library issues. Back then, however, I could claim some slender thread of credibility, since I was in the midst of a two-year hitch as Interim University Librarian at the University of Minnesota. Today I haven't even that slender thread to cling to, for I write not as a librarian-manqué, but as a faculty member and historian!

As I scanned the Virtually Yours Institute roster, moreover, I found that, with perhaps one exception, I was to be the sole non-librarian on the program. That realization brought to mind the old saw about Christopher Columbus, who long ago also ventured into unfamiliar terrain: that he didn't know where he was going when he set out; didn't know where he was when he arrived; and didn't know where he'd been when he got home! I hope that my brief sortie back into the world of librarianship won't prove quite so confounding.

Fortunately there is reason to hope that it will not, since I continue to have both a close association with and a deep respect for research libraries and their staffs. At Minnesota, I am closely dependent on my librarian colleagues for my own work. From my days as University Librarian, I carried away a continuing interest in the central, often problematic, and constantly evolving place that libraries occupy as information providers in academic settings.

As I turned to the task of preparing this chapter, I wondered what I might most usefully have to say concerning the "Evolving Responsibilities for Managing Electronic Resources and Services." I am clearly in no position to speak to the myriad technical questions generated by the continuing revolution in information technologies. Nor can I meaningfully address the question of how library staffs should be arrayed to serve their clients more effectively in today's complex, evolving electronic environment.

What I can offer are some personal observations on the electronic revolution that continues to transform our professional lives, observations launched from the perspective of a deeply interested and reasonably informed user of academic libraries and their information systems. There are, of course, dangers in professing to speak as a "typical" library user, for, as you know only too well, we users differ, often very substantially, by virtue of the fields of knowledge in which we work, fields in which information is structured, accessed, and communicated in very different ways; by the kinds of institutions with which we are associated, given their contrasting clienteles and educational missions; by our different information needs as faculty, graduate or undergraduate students, or members of the general public; as well as by our on-campus or at-a-distance locations. In sharp contrast to the visual wizardry that on TV allows one human visage to be electronically morphed into another, library users remain doggedly, even at times defiantly different from each other. Certainly my own perspective on library issues is shaped by who I am, by the kind of work that I do, and by the kind of institution that I call home. Of the many observations that I might make, I'll be content to offer but two. As you will see, they are closely related.[1]

The first of them goes something like this. The penetration of our colleges and universities by new information and communication technologies promises, on the one hand, to bind our institutional communities more closely together. For better or worse, and I sometimes wonder which it is, we exchange countless messages via the remarkably efficient device of e-mail. At our home institutions, moreover, many of us can access a seemingly limitless array of institutional information, not only from our offices but from virtually anywhere on campus, while electronic discussion groups allow committee members to communicate with each other between meetings, or even without holding formal meetings (a form of "virtual conferencing" with which we are all familiar). In many ways, then, the new technologies we use serve to strengthen intellectual exchange and social community on our campuses.

Yet they serve at the same time to weaken institutional focus and commitment by carrying our energies and attention away from our home institutions to wider communities, real as well as virtual, of students, scholars, and librarians. I want to talk briefly about that.

One of the central, defining themes of American academic life during the past fifty years has been the loss of cohesion, of a meaningful and effective sense of community within our institutions of higher learning. Certainly that has been true in large public universities such as my own. I imagine it has happened in other colleges and universities, as well. The explanations for this basic transformation in what might be termed the civic character of American higher education are many, but surely they include:

> the greater cultural richness and social diversity of our faculties, staffs, and student bodies (itself a wonderful, democratic development);

> the increasing proliferation and specialization of academic fields of inquiry that have complicated the language of scholarly discourse and in many cases narrowed the orbit of academic interaction;

> the increasing professionalization of both faculty and librarians' lives that has strengthened our orientation toward and commitment to national and international associations;

> the vast growth since World War II of off-campus funding for scholarly research and other academic programming, including the work of librarians, especially by the government but by business and private foundations as well, with the multiple dependencies and channels of accountability that such funding creates.

No doubt other circumstances have been at work as well.

It seems clear that one important effect of our emerging information and communication technologies will be to strengthen, even accelerate, these dissipative institutional tendencies by connecting us across space, via the Internet and other networks of communication, to virtual electronic communities lying beyond our campus boundaries. While such networks expand our professional horizons and enrich our intellectual lives, they also call into question our commitments of time and loyalty to the academic communities that we happen to call home.

The decentering effect of information technologies is evident as well in the speed and facility with which they can be made to serve the distinctive informational needs of diverse scholarly communities, communities within which inquiry is organized, knowledge is structured, and the conventions of professional communication are arranged in fundamentally different ways. Even while the informational needs of historians and biologists, engineers and legal scholars, laboratory scientists and medical clinicians are being satisfied, these divergent communities grow more distant from each other.

The consequences for librarians of this explosive divergence in information systems are both obvious and troubling, for information providers are expected not only to understand the intellectual grounding of such divergencies, but to make strategic choices among a constantly changing array of technologies, choices always restricted by inadequate collections and technology budgets. It's a difficult enough assignment at small, relatively compact liberal arts colleges. How much more daunting it proves to be at complex universities such as my own, even with their larger and more specialized library staffs. The academic communities we inhabit, I'm afraid, are likely to become more intellectually fractured and socially weakened as the electronic revolution proceeds.

My second set of observations follows from what I have already said. Librarians and their patron/clients have always been closely dependent on each other, partners, to borrow a metaphor from Peggy Johnson, in an intimate informational dance. While closely dependent on each other, those of us participating in this dance—librarians and faculty, students, and the general public—often step on each others' toes. We do so because we bring to it not only different styles but different needs. As librarians and teaching/research faculty, we differ in our professional ambitions and responsibilities, our day-to-day activities, and in the performance standards by which we are judged. It is my impression that the continuing, seemingly endless revolution in information technologies on which we are inescapably embarked is further testing our long-established and essential partnership. In what ways might that be so?

In earlier times (were they really simpler, or do they only seem so in retrospect?), working relationships between bibliographers and faculty, between reference librarians and their various clients were more stable, which is to say more mutually understood, in large part because the ways in which information was structured and the processes by which it was accessed were less diverse and more broadly familiar. In recent years, those relationships, those strategies of negotiation between information users and information providers, have been altered in problematic if fascinating ways.

For one thing, librarians differ in their commitment to and mastery over the awesome electronic agenda that Clifford Lynch and Ross Atkinson have so forcefully described, as well as over their role as mediators between information sources and their users. At the same time, faculty and other library users are similarly divided in their openness to new information systems, as well as in their ability to negotiate those systems on their own. Beyond that, there is an expanding universe of information services and specialists, accessible via the Internet from home and office, lying beyond the physical confines, organizational structures, and management responsibilities of academic libraries. There are, as well, multiple information utilities on our own campuses whose missions often overlap and who eagerly compete for political and financial support.

Now it may be that we are presently caught in a unique, short-term technological time warp, that we are presently passing through a particularly jarring threshold that will, in time, usher us onto calmer technological seas and provide more stable parameters within which more gradual change will occur. A glance backward at the introduction of earlier, similarly transformative communication technologies—print, for example, or the telegraph or telephone—offers some support for such a belief. In my more sober moments, however, I have my doubts. Those doubts, I feel compelled to say, have been deepened by contemplating the endlessly unfolding, even accelerating future sketched so powerfully for us by Ross Atkinson.

It also may be the case, which seems perhaps more likely, that as the generational cycle among librarians, faculty, and other library users continues its inexorable turn, greater familiarity with and agreement concerning the management of electronic technologies will emerge. At least we can hope so. Whatever the case, the negotiation of this constantly shifting technological terrain by users and providers alike promises to be intense and difficult at least in the immediate future. Above all, it needs to go forward carefully and with the full participation of all whose interests are deeply involved. If it's true that war is too important to be left to the generals, decisions about managing the technologies currently transforming our professional lives are too important to be left solely in the hands of their most committed advocates.

None of us intend to be left behind in the technological sweepstakes on which we are embarked. And yet the constancy of technological change, even as it opens new horizons and enriches our professional lives, also can be immensely disruptive for librarians and patrons alike. We must, of course, embrace innovations that enhance our capacity to provide essential information services, and that thus serve the fundamental teaching and research missions of our institutions. Our professional responsibilities, as faculty and librarians, require it, while administrators frequently demand it. Yet let me hazard the thought that we must at the same time avoid the intellectual, programmatic, and fiscal trap of imagining that we must perpetually live on the ever expanding, always exhausting leading edge of technological exploration and change. While such a strenuous existence may prove exhilarating to those most deeply invested in its perpetuation, it has the capacity not so much to serve as to continuously disrupt the processes of scholarship and teaching that are, after all, the fundamental purposes to be served.

How, of course, are we to locate the boundary between serving and disrupting the essential processes of scholarship and learning, between improvements that further basic institutional missions and "improvements" that are driven by a narrower technological agenda? Different participants in this complicated

dance—faculty and other information users, librarians, administrators, afi-
cionados of information science and their attendant technologies, each of them
reflecting distinctive viewpoints and priorities—will surely draw those boundaries differently. It is thus essential that a full range of voices participate in the
dialogue through which such critical decisions are made.

At best this is certain to prove a complicated task, one filled with shifting
signals not unlike that encountered by the old man who, as the ancient fable
goes, found himself traveling toward a market town accompanied by his son
and a donkey that they intended to sell. The road they traversed was muddy
and difficult, and so the old man rode on the donkey's back while his son
trudged wearily alongside. In time they met a stranger who angrily asked the
old man if he was not ashamed to ride by himself and allow his son to slog un-
happily through the mire. This so embarrassed the old man that he took his
son up behind him, and they rode on together. They had not traveled far when
another stranger exclaimed that the man and his son were both unmerciful
beggars for riding on the back of such a poor beast. Whereupon the old man
got down and let his son ride on alone. Well, as you might anticipate, in a short
while they encountered a third traveler who called the son a "graceless, ras-
cally, young jackanapes" for riding while his aged father trudged through the
dirt, and called the old man a fool for allowing it in the bargain! And so the
harried old man called his son down, and they walked ahead together leading
the donkey by his halter, until, as luck would have it, they encountered a final
traveler who called both of them senseless blockheads for going on foot while
leading an animal on which they might ride. Finally, the old man could stand
the harassment no longer and, turning to his son, declared: "It grieves me that
we cannot please all these people. Let us throw the donkey over the next
bridge and be no further troubled with him."

Well, we can't throw the shimmering new electronic donkey over the bridge
and have done with it, even if at times it seems an attractive option. But neither,
as the fable suggests, can we react to every conflicting sentiment and cross-
cutting pressure we encounter. In each of our institutions, priorities have to be
set by way of charting a consistent and reasonable course. Above all, we have
to go forward together: librarians eager to keep abreast of their profession; faculty and other library users intent upon the tasks of teaching and research; administrators given to groaning not only about the fiscal "black hole" of
acquisitions but increasingly about technological "black holes" as well; and the
managers of other information utilities on our campuses, also players in the
high stakes, broadly distributed information environment in which we work.

If our decisions are to serve our educational priorities effectively, and above
all if they are to be supportable over time, they must emerge from a vigorous,

4

Reconceptualizing Partnerships

Deanna B. Marcum

Once, on a trip abroad, I met with several librarians and scientists with responsibilities for preservation. As I nearly always do in the United States, I ended each meeting with the question, "Can you think of any ways our two organizations might cooperate?" One scientist, who had devoted years to understanding the threats of bugs and pests to book paper, immediately responded, "Yes, I have a very good suggestion for cooperation. You have money. I have a research lab that desperately needs money. You give us money, and we will do our research. This is very good cooperation."

In this case, language difficulties exaggerated the blunt message, but, in fact, all too often when we talk about cooperation and partnerships, these are simply code words for "we need more money." I believe using the word *partnerships* to mean that we'll go to great lengths to secure money is both "old school" thinking and counterproductive.

Partnerships has become the requisite password for getting any attention from an external funding agency. The more cynical among us point out that even the not-for-profit organizations have bought into the power of this buzzword, and partnerships are created as an act of showmanship. However, a less cynical and equally compelling view is that external funders have begun to understand the power of digital technology for providing access to information resources, and they know that, through partnerships, even small projects easily can be amplified to bring benefits to many new and often unanticipated audiences. The funding agencies understand that the political, social, and cultural climates in which all of us operate demand that we leverage our individual efforts by combining forces with other institutions and agencies.

Partnerships in the digital environment are quite different from those we have known in the past. In the days of interlibrary loan, for example, we were more concerned about the big libraries being overtaken by requests from the little ones. In that environment, we formed partnerships with institutions of similar size and funding level, or we grouped ourselves by state when tax money was used as an incentive for creating partnerships, or we grouped ourselves along subject discipline lines. Humanities librarians found other humanities librarians with whom to work so that users of both institutions might benefit. Today, partnerships are often mandatory because we as a profession do not possess or control, generally speaking, the web of hardware, software, legal rights, or content ownership needed to provide services to certain categories of electronic information without joining forces with commercial services and content providers. Thus, in a purely practical sense, the technology forces collaboration with partners that have heretofore been strangers.

These partnerships—admittedly, sometimes of the shotgun variety—need not be painful or trying, but without careful thought at the onset, they will be. I will describe some of the partnerships that have been particularly productive and others that have experienced problems. From these case studies I then will draw some conclusions about the requirements for effective partnerships.

Large-Scale Partnerships with the Commercial Sector

Among the many efforts to build digital library collections, the Library of Congress' National Digital Library Program is the most visible and largest. When the Librarian of Congress, James Billington, realized the improbability of receiving extra Congressional appropriations for converting the LC collections to digital form, he and the staff developed a plan to appeal to private, commercial interests. LC crafted a plan to digitize five million items from the historical collections that document the formation and growth of the nation and to distribute these collections through a widely available medium—the World Wide Web.

With a budget projection of $60 million for the project, the Library of Congress mounted an enormous fund-raising effort—called the "partnerships campaign"—to raise $45 million from private sources as matching funds for the $15 million that Congress pledged. The fund-raising campaign was much strengthened by the fact that LC had experience in digitizing historical primary sources. The American Memory project—with its relatively modest congressional funding—had produced CD-ROMs of topical interest. In creating these products, LC had gained practical experience in digitizing text, photographs, music, motion picture clips, and recorded speeches. The staff had learned through sometimes painful trial and error which vendors had the capability to undertake digital conversion projects. They had gained a significant knowledge of resolution standards for materials in various formats.

In my view, the most important decision that the Library of Congress made in organizing its partnerships campaign was to emphasize its benefits to new audiences. The service policy of the Library of Congress limits access to adults over the age of eighteen with a "serious research interest." This policy had been established many years before—both to keep local school groups out of the already busy reading rooms and to protect the rare and unique materials from deterioration through over-use. But by converting important historical materials to electronic forms, the digital surrogates were easily available to schoolchildren everywhere.

Commercial contributors who responded to this solicitation could take justifiable pride in helping to make these important national documents widely accessible. They also could take pride in a project that promised to improve education—a need that is recognized by all sectors of the society. Finally—and significantly—a contribution of any amount would move the project closer to completion. No single contribution would mean the success or failure of the overall programs. The Library of Congress established a calendar for meeting the goal of five million images. Each contribution is duly acknowledged and appreciated, without tying ownership of a specific phase of the project or a particular collection to a funding partner.

For this strategy to work, LC had to identify the collections to be digitized. Standards and best practices had to be agreed to—at least for a point of time—so that actual work could be started once funds were in hand.

The critical element was the establishment of an educational outreach section at LC. Six individuals with experience in and connections to the K-12 educational community were hired to conduct workshops and institutes for teachers, both to make them aware of the digital resources that are now available through the LC National Digital Library Program and to learn more from them about how images need to be presented to be most useful to the K-12 audience.

The Digital Library Federation

A very different kind of partnership development is seen in the Digital Library Federation, a loose collaboration of seventeen research libraries, all of which have active digital library projects under way and all of which are committed to the development of standards, systems architecture, and metadata that allow for interoperability.

These institutions did not set out to form a partnership of any kind. Rather, they fell into it. The Commission on Preservation and Access had funded a few institutions to experiment with digital technology for preservation purposes. While carrying out their projects, several of the principal investigators concluded that they should meet as a group to discuss the ramifications of their work. They suggested to the Commission on Preservation and Access that the individual institutions should work together to think about how digital libraries will function. A small group of library directors, calling themselves the La Guardia Six, began to meet informally to discuss the implications of digital technology. The group grew to eight and then twelve. The common thread was that each institution had been funded by the Commission on Preservation and Access.

Recognizing that they needed to become more focused if they wanted to engage in collaborative projects, the group agreed to work on a document that outlined how members might cooperate on digital projects. A subset produced a document, issued in March 1994, which proposed the formation of the Digital Preservation Consortium, a group of universities dedicated to working together so that researchers and students in various university environments across the country and around the world can make the most effective use of library materials preserved in digital form. Through the joint efforts of its members, the mission of the consortium was to advance the use and utility of digital technology for preserving and improving access to intellectual works of national and international importance.

Shortly after the consortium was formed, the Library of Congress announced its intention to create a National Digital Library. In its announcements, LC indicated a desire to work with others in the library community to build a virtual collection of documents relating to America's history. The university members of the Digital Preservation Consortium realized that many of their goals were identical or similar to the stated goals of the Library of Congress initiative. The Commission on Preservation and Access staff approached LC on behalf of the consortium members to consider participation in the consortium. Further discussions raised the possibility of the National Archives also joining the project. When the group reconvened to consider what it should do collectively, it gave itself the name the National Digital Library Federation. Its members decided to keep the group small and flexible, largely because they believed that only a small, relatively cohesive group could make progress quickly. Always there was the intention to expand the group once it became practical to do so.

This case study of partnerships is particularly interesting because it raises issues about exclusiveness that trouble many in our profession. The group of a dozen or so institutions believed (rightly or wrongly) that they were at the forefront of digital library development in the research university community. They believed they could—indeed, were obliged to—make progress in a few areas for the benefit of the wider library community. Not surprisingly, the act of working as a self-selected small group was offensive to other members of the library community. For all their good intentions, and even though the participating libraries were financing the federation, the group had alienated colleagues who had the same interests, even if not the same resources.

The National Digital Library Federation is now the Digital Library Federation, partly to blunt the grandiosity of the name, but also to indicate that this is not a national program. Rather, it is an activity, probably with international dimensions, to find ways to enable institutions to exchange the products of their digital library projects. Directors of some of the most active digital library projects understood that several things needed to happen to assure interoperability of digital libraries. Work must be done to create a common system architecture, develop common discovery and retrieval mechanisms, and assure the preservation of digital information. Participants in the federation also now understand that partnerships that appear to be formed in secret, even if for the best reasons, are likely to face serious problems. Since June of this year, we have opened participation in the federation to all libraries that have active digital projects under way, are willing to invest their own resources in the program at the same rate as the charter members, and are willing to have their staff engaged in cooperative projects. We have corrected many of the problems that existed previously, but we may be suffering for quite a long time from the perception that we tried to form an exclusive "club." I am relating this case study as a cautionary tale about the way in which partnerships are formed.

Despite many of the organizational problems experienced by the group, the federation is an excellent example of library-corporation partnerships that are necessary in the digital environment. Even large and well-funded institutions cannot create a digital library capacity on their own. To effectively address the problems of system architecture, discovery and retrieval mechanisms, and digital preservation, members of the corporate community also must be involved. Standards can be realized only when there is substantial participation in the development process and ultimate "buy-in" by the commercial sector. The federation simply cannot achieve its goals without forming partnerships with technology and telecommunications groups.

The Council on Library and Information Resources

The final case study I will describe is one about which I cannot be entirely objective. The Council on Library and Information Resources, the organization for which I am responsible, is built on an elaborate structure of partnerships. It is the product of a recent merger of the Council on Library Resources and the Commission on Preservation and Access. The older organization, the Council on Library Resources, was established in 1956 with $5 million from the Ford Foundation. Until 1976, the council was funded exclusively by the Ford Foundation. It was quite a simple and lovely formula: every five years another check for $5 million was deposited in the checking account. Ford had established the council, in part, for its own purposes. The foundation was receiving many proposals for automating university libraries (in those days automation referred to punch card operations for circulation and inventory control). Rather than hiring specialists in library matters for the Ford Foundation staff, the foundation officers decided setting up an organization devoted to library matters would be more expedient. With assurances that more money would be available on a predictable schedule, the Council on Library Resources, with its separate board of mostly scholars and academic officers, felt reasonably secure in offering grant funds to institutions that presented the best research ideas or that proposed projects that needed to be undertaken for the common good. The role of the board was to choose the best from among the many ideas presented to it.

By 1976, the Ford Foundation had made many changes in its internal processes and notified the council that it would no longer be a sole provider of CLR funds. Other funding sources would have to be identified, and the president of the council needed to articulate a longer-term program and make presentations to foundations for operating monies. After Warren J. Haas was named president in 1978, he created an informal body called the Foundation Library Committee to discuss the overarching needs of the research library community. He convened once or twice a year the presidents of the largest foundations known to have an interest in libraries and presented them with a big-picture view of where libraries were headed. He presented ideas for national programs that would be helpful and attached budgets to them for consideration by the foundation presidents. Out of these gatherings grew such initiatives as the Bibliographic Services Development Program, which brought the Library of Congress, OCLC, and RLG together to discuss the universal accessibility of bibliographic records, and a national preservation microfilming program that called for a coordinated effort to preserve a portion of the collections held in American research libraries.

These large-scale national programs had some features in common: they were coordinated by the Council on Library Resources, money was made available to CLR by the large private foundations for further distribution to individual institutions, and progress was measured by the level of participation in a national effort rather than by individual institutional accomplishments.

The Commission on Preservation and Access had quite a different beginning. Preservation had been a CLR program from its earliest days in 1956. In 1985, CLR, in a alliance with the Association of American Universities, formed task forces of scholars, administrators, and librarians to consider the most pressing problems of the research library. Among them was a task force on preservation. The group of scholars and librarians who considered the problem urged that there be special attention paid to the problem of deteriorating library materials. From their very strong recommendation, a separate organization with its own working board was created to bring the problem of brittle books to the attention of a much broader audience and to stimulate federal funding for a national effort to preserve library materials. The documentary film *Slow Fires* was created for public television audiences. It was used in many different venues to create a sense of urgency and to stimulate public financing of preservation microfilming. The National Endowment for the Humanities agreed to establish a separate funding line for preservation of library materials, and every year, testimony on the progress of the preservation program was offered.

The Commission on Preservation and Access was formed not as an operating foundation but as a public charity with the purpose of raising public awareness of and stimulating funding for preservation. Instead of relying on foundation funding for the organization, the commission established a group of sponsoring institutions. Nine research universities with extensive preservation programs of their own were asked to sponsor the commission with a $25,000 annual payment. Using these sponsorship fees as the operating base for the organization, the commission then could go to foundations and ask for project money exclusively. The commission worked with a small number of handpicked institutions to identify the projects that would advance the national preservation agenda, institutions were asked to take on work that had been identified by the commission board, and reports were made available to the sponsors at no cost and to the rest of the library and scholarly community for a very low fee.

As interest in the commission's work spread, there was an eventual broadening in the base of sponsorship, to the point that now any library with an interest in supporting preservation work is invited to become a sponsor. For the large research institutions, the fee is $3,000 per year, but the fee for smaller institutions is on a sliding scale and goes as low as $500 per year for college libraries. The Commission on Preservation and Access is now a program of the Council on Library and Information Resources (CLIR), but it continues to operate from the monies contributed by sponsors, and we have tried to make the case to the library community that all libraries have a stake in supporting preservation programs.

When the boards of the Council on Library Resources and the Commission on Preservation and Access decided that the time was right to merge the two organizations at the beginning of 1995, they had specific concerns about the need to form new partnerships and alliances. My review of the new organization's objectives will help explain how we view partnerships these days.

In some ways, the first partnership—two organizations agreeing to share a president—was the hardest. Each of the organizations had a proud history, a strong and independent board, and its own staff. By agreeing to first affiliate and then merge, each gave up some of its autonomy in order to achieve cost savings and program unification. This was not nearly as difficult to achieve organizationally as it was emotionally. In any organization, no matter how small, a culture takes hold that defines staff work habits, organizational directions and priorities, and ways of communicating with the outside world. All of these internal preferences were subject to questioning and revision when the two organizations became one.

Our second adjustment came in thinking about funding sources. Whether we liked it or not, we had to acknowledge that almost no foundations were any longer willing to cover the operating costs of a small not-for-profit organization, no matter how important its work. Although difficult from an organizational planning perspective, our future funding almost certainly will come from two sources: relatively small amounts from sponsorship fees and larger funds for specific projects from the private foundations. To secure these funds, we must become entrepreneurial, opportunistic, and highly flexible. The not-so-positive side is that staff have little or no security. Only the strong and courageous will find CLIR a desirable work environment.

The third adjustment is that despite our historical efforts to steer clear of commercial interests, we must form partnerships with the technology and business communities. Several of our programs dictate an involvement with them. In the digital environment, there are many fewer projects that libraries can undertake and maintain independently. As soon as we move from the ownership model for collection development to a model of providing access to information from highly disparate sources, libraries automatically enter into new partnerships. The same is true for our small think-tank organization. In order to work on standards for system interoperability, we are required to form strong alliances with the technology vendors. We need their money, of course, but much more than that we need their expertise and their willingness to involve systems designers in our discussions about library needs.

This is a difficult partnership to master. Our past experiences with the vendor community have bred suspicion on both sides. We have to rise above that suspicion and doubt and enter into working agreements for mutual benefit. To do this requires new skills, new ways of managing projects, and far more involvement with technically competent staff from different types of libraries. Increasingly, our budget is spent on meetings with representatives from many different communities.

The partnerships we are developing with the scholarly community are just as difficult in another way. CLIR has joined in partnership with the American Council of Learned Societies to create task forces on the humanities and digital technology. We understand that many faculty have serious questions about investments in the technology at the expense of more traditional library collections. Instead of trying to persuade the scholarly community that librarians have the digital situation under control, we have formed small groups of librarians and scholars to explore what libraries must do to ensure that scholars will have access to the information resources they need to do their work in the digital environment.

All of these partnerships require a special kind of program staff. In the old days of CLR, the staff consisted of librarians who could evaluate proposals. They brought their knowledge of the library community to bear on the ideas presented to them, worked with the proposing institutions to modify the projects or streamline the budgets, and monitored project expenses and results. Today, the CLIR program staff (who are themselves from many different disciplines) must have very good ideas of their own. They must know well the library, the scholarly, and the technology communities, or they must have connections that will take them to those communities as needed. The staff must be able to set priorities and stick with them. We must be able to ignore many of the good ideas presented to us while always keeping an open mind.

Another important skill is the ability to focus. CLIR has a small staff and limited resources; we cannot do an excellent job if we take on too many projects—even if there are many needs. Working with the Board of Directors, we reduced the many possibilities to four program areas: the Commission on Preservation and Access, Digital Libraries, Economics of Information, and Leadership. We are able to magnify the effects a small staff can have by engaging organizational and individual partners in each of the program areas.

The Commission on Preservation and Access has solicited 108 institutional sponsors. With a relatively small amount of money annually from each sponsor, we can assure sustained attention to preservation issues. The Digital Library Federation also has institutional participants, but in this case, the institutions contribute a larger amount to cover the costs of program staff and to operate projects. In the Economics of Information program, we have formed a partnership with Coopers & Lybrand, an international financial management firm. We want to learn more about how resources are allocated for providing information resources across a campus. In the digital environment, information comes from many sources other than the library. What is the effect of the digital environment on the investments made in providing information for the campus community? We were able to interest Coopers & Lybrand in helping us develop a study to find some of the answers to our questions by showing them how working with us on the project could lead to product development for their company. In the Leadership program, we are working with Emory University to develop a Digital Leadership Institute for managers of information resources—librarians, computing center directors, university press directors, and bookstore managers—on campuses. From consulting widely with such individuals on a variety of campuses, we came to realize the need for such an institute, but we are too small to organize courses and follow up practicum projects. We realized that we must work with a university with the resources to deliver instructional programs.

Effective Partnerships

This paper has presented several different types of partnerships. I have identified some of the things that have worked, as well as some that were not quite so successful. The main point I wish to make is that partnerships are effective only when they fit with the overall mission of the organization. They cannot be grafted on to an existing operation only to provide much needed capital. Partnerships cannot be set in motion without changing the very nature of the existing organizations.

As the Commission and Council Boards were discussing what the results of a merger would be, each group announced that it thinks of the organization as a catalyst. After several minutes of discussing the virtues of catalytic agents, one of the scientists in the group pointed out that we should aim much higher. A catalyst, he said, is a substance that increases the rate of chemical reaction, without being affected itself.

Instead of being a catalyst organization, we have sought to become a partnership organization. Old formulas for funding are not available to us any longer. We have to use our relatively small amounts of money as an investment in projects that are managed collaboratively with other organizations that also have small amounts of money. We recognize that we give up a lot of control in the process, but if we make careful, strategic investments in the partnerships, we can achieve our most important goals.

PART II

Understanding User Needs in a Changing Environment

5

Virtually Yours: Models for Managing Electronic Resources and Services

Bonnie MacEwan

One of the most interesting and exciting aspects of building digital collections is the impact these new ways of providing information have had on the way librarians are organized to do their work. In order to meet the challenges and take advantage of the many opportunities of this new environment, we have had to learn to be more flexible and agile in the way we are organized for collection development and library services. The rules, procedures, and standard practices that have guided us so well in the past have to be quickly changed to adapt to the new and ever-changing environment. There are some real similarities between the agility required to develop collections and provide services today and the way the cartoon characters Calvin and Hobbes feel about organized sports. One recurring theme in the cartoon series has to do with Calvin's thoughts about the rules and structure of baseball. He finds all of the many rules stifling and far prefers a game he and Hobbes created and named, Calvinball. As Hobbes tells us in several of the comic strips, "No sport is less organized than Calvinball!"[1] In fact, Calvinball's greatest virtue is that it is a studied effort to introduce constant variety and variation of the rules.

There are strong similarities between Calvinball and a good collection development program. In fact, collection development has already enjoyed a long history of flexible organizational patterns. Often job responsibilities have evolved that are responsive to change and the needs of the organization rather than following some preset model. As Bonnie Bryant's work on organizational models for collection development documented, numerous models for collection development exist and succeed in academic libraries.[2] Recent work by Peggy Johnson indicates that this is still the case.[3] There are many models and most of them function effectively. Some libraries have a highly centralized organization, while others are very decentralized. Librarians may be designated as subject and area bibliographers or be members of loosely coordinated groups with broad assignments. In some libraries there are small, exclusive collection development staffs, and in others many librarians hold selection responsibilities. In some libraries there are elaborate committee structures to gather advice from academic units. One high-level administrator may be responsible for managing collection development, or several points of management, distributed by large subject areas, may operate. What seems to be most important is that the structure responds to the needs of the organization and corresponds to the skills of the librarians. Nancy Cline suggests we shift our focus from the departmental program of collection development and focus on the skills, leadership abilities, and capabilities needed for the future of collection development.[4]

Clifford Lynch reminds us that scholarly publication and communication are going through major changes. These changes are driven by the economics of both the publishing industry and higher education, the availability of electronic formats as alternate delivery mechanisms, and the changing nature of research and scholarship in the academic disciplines. The ways information can be exchanged electronically are evolving every day. These developments are changing the means by which libraries provide services to faculty and students who are dependent on access to raw data, primary sources, and the varied products of scholarly exchange. It is very difficult for librarians to keep up with these many changes. However, it is essential that collection strategies not only keep pace but continue to look forward and plan for the future.

As collection development moves into this new environment, the organization for collection development will matter even less than it has in the past. What will matter most are the abilities of those responsible for collection development. Identifying exactly who is involved in collection development will continue to shift and change as the meaning of what it is to develop collections changes over time. There is a strong need for public services librarians to connect what they know about the users with their needs. This argues for a strong connection, perhaps even a merging, of collection development and public services.

In many libraries the cataloging departments find themselves holding an unexpected collection development debate as they implement the new 856 MARC field. This field will allow for hot links directly from the catalog record to the electronic version of the work. So the collection development question is, should the cataloger make a link to the electronic version of the thing itself, in essence both selecting and acquiring the electronic version of the title? This is a debate that both lies far outside the traditional debate of "who selects" and shifts it to what the competencies needed for selection are. In 1994, Nancy Cline provided a list of competencies that is still useful.[5] Her list of competencies includes specific collections related strengths such as: knowledge of technology and licensing issues; an understanding of users' technological needs and how they interact with resources; a broad knowledge of publishing and the economics of publishing; and a good grasp of scholarly communications issues such as commitment to the freedom of access to information and respect for diverse points of view. Many of the competencies on her list are much broader in nature. They include a commitment to change, innovation, and creativity; a commitment to professionalism; the ability to reason analytically; being adaptable, flexible, and resilient; being a visionary; the ability to think strategically; being resourceful; excellent communication skills; a keen sense of political contexts; knowledge of higher education and research needs; tolerance for ambiguity; commitment to resource sharing; and a strong subject knowledge. At this point, she admits that the list is a "pretty tall order" and adds the ability to spin gold from straw. Clearly, this list of competencies suggests a librarian who is able to change quickly, has a good grasp of all aspects of the working environment and of the publishing world, and has good general work skills. It suggests someone who can begin playing our own form of "Calvinball" whenever the occasion calls for this level of flexibility and agility.

The emerging emphasis on electronic resources, the need for inter-institutional resource sharing, and changes in scholarly communication place collection development in a constantly shifting environment. The leadership for collection development and those who select and provide services for these resources must be agile enough to make sense of this environment that changes constantly. In many ways, we play Calvinball. As soon as we hit an obstacle or a seemingly insurmountable challenge, we must be prepared to change course, create a new rule, a new approach, or just plain make something up that works in this particular case.

Our users need us to build coherent and useful collections for the future. To accomplish this effectively, libraries will have to invest in continuous staff development. It will be vital that there is a shared understanding of the vision, the values, and the priorities of the institution. If each individual responsible for collection development and service holds these in common, the particular organizational structure will be less important. Our work to serve the public must inform our collection building and our work to build the collection must inform our services in an endless loop and a never-ending changing pattern.

Services and selection will increasingly become two sides of the same coin; the difference between them is already so diminished that the relationship informs everything we do in collection development and in services. As we build Web pages, we are selecting resources, and as we select Web-based resources, we will be building and delivering instruction and information services for our users.

Librarians find themselves in the midst of very exciting and changing times. Some of the changes may seem more positive than others. The breakdown in the clear distinction in roles in our libraries is one of the positives of the many changes. The opportunity to work collaboratively with everyone in the library and the university to build excellent collections and to deliver excellent services is one of the most exciting developments of recent years. Additionally, we now have the ability to work collaboratively with librarians regardless of location to build collections and offer services. The health sciences librarians in the Committee on Institutional Cooperation (CIC) have worked collaboratively to build informative Web pages (http://healthweb.org/) that are serving the needs of users at all thirteen locations of the CIC and in fact all over the world. Similarly, Penn State's business librarians at all of our locations worked together to jointly build Web pages to serve the users throughout the twenty-three locations of Penn State. They are building on the experience of the criminal justice selectors at two Penn State locations who worked together to build a single electronic collection to serve users at all locations. On the national level, the agriculture librarians are designing a project called AgNIC (http://www.agnic.org/) to build Web pages of agricultural information and offer specialized reference services.

Many, although not yet all, of our users are ready to use these resources in creative and innovative ways to improve their teaching and research. Part of our challenge is to design services and to build collections for those who are eager to embrace electronic resources while meeting the needs of users who are not quite ready for them. Unlike Calvin and Hobbes, who have a rule that you never do the same thing twice, we must continue to do some of what we have always done while moving enthusiastically forward with the new. We must play excellent baseball and excellent Calvinball at the same time. That's a rule that might well challenge Calvin and Hobbes.

The best news of all is the assurance that we already have most of the skills to accomplish these goals. Most of the skills, talents, and abilities we brought to our work to provide services and select resources in "traditional formats" are just as important in building the virtual library. We bring to our work both the key skills and an understanding of what libraries are about. "If you can trust your decisions in the traditional world, you can build a digital library."[6] If we have flexible and creative organizations and approach our work with collaboration, flexibility, and creativity, we can meet our evolving responsibilities. Perhaps we can even avoid the punishment for violating the rules of Calvinball and we will not have to sing the "Very Sorry Song."

Notes

1. Bill Watterson, *Scientific Progress Goes "Boink"* (Kansas City, Mo.: Andrews & McMeel, 1991), 101.
2. Bonita Bryant, "The Organizational Structure of Collection Development," *Library Resources & Technical Services* 31 (April/June 1987): 118.
3. Conversations with Peggy Johnson about her research on collection development organizations.
4. Nancy M. Cline, "Staffing: The Art of Managing Change," in *Collection Management and Development: Issues in an Electronic Era,* ed. Peggy Johnson and Bonnie MacEwan (Chicago: American Library Association, 1994): 14.
5. Ibid., 25.
6. Karen G. Schneider, "Internet Librarian: A Nice Little Digital Library," *American Libraries* 28 (October 1997): 76.

6

Assessment:
How and Why

Gloriana St. Clair

In May 1998, the *Journal of Academic Librarianship* devoted an entire issue to papers on assessment with a lead article by Ronald F. Dow, outlining theory and detailing applications at the University of Rochester.[1] This issue reflects the growing concern libraries have with assessing their own practices as a part of a larger university emphasis on issues of analysis and accountability. My thesis in this chapter is that collections officers need to be paying attention to the nature of their jobs and that they can increase effectiveness through an active program of assessment.

Only through ongoing effective assessment can collections officers meet the evolving needs of new technologies and new generations of students and faculty. This paper covers two general areas—why do assessment and how to do it.

The thinking about assessment discussed here evolves from a set of assumptions. These assumptions are:

- Collection development is changing rapidly.
- By 2020, 50 percent of information will be electronic.
- All libraries accept the access paradigm.
- Local buying employs Ross Atkinson's ideas as expounded in his paper in this collected proceedings and in many of his articles about what should be purchased locally and what can be used through the access system.[2]

Most collections officers understand how rapidly their field is changing and are vigorously pursuing various methods to keep their skills current with the challenges inherent in the position. The rate of change in the scholarly communications system is difficult for anyone to predict. The 2020 50 percent figure serves merely as an indication of how pervasive the change might be and what the possible timing would be. This is probably optimistic. While all librarians do not accept the access paradigm, most have had to work in that environment for a number of years and understand those trade-offs. From this evolving situation, ideas about what should be owned locally are being formed, and more and more librarians are studying the dimensions of their local demand and the areas in which access can be a relatively satisfactory alternative.

Why Do Assessment?

Assessment is done to satisfy the requirements of various audiences whose needs are changing. Academic libraries have services whose audiences have turned elsewhere. Paper indexes now often sit deserted. Their audience has moved over to the electronic versions of those indexes and to the World Wide Web browsers. Four important audiences for assessment efforts are college and university administrators, faculty, students, and other librarians.

College and University Administrators

University and college administrators have several complicated and sophisticated interests in understanding the relative merit of their institution's collections. These have been summarized around the topics of reputation, equity, and bragging rights.

Reputation

Like other members of the academic community, administrators are interested in their institution's reputation nationally and within their peer group. Most of the reputational measures in use now are measures of quantity. For instance, the Association for Research Libraries measures quantity exclusively. The ranking index that appears annually in the *Chronicle for Higher Education* uses a formula based on number of volumes held, number of serials subscriptions, number of added volumes, number of staff, and total number of dollars. Smaller university and college ranking schemes tend to use the same data—all of which is quantitative. None of these data measure the effectiveness of the library in meeting the programmatic needs of the college or university. Standard measures do not compute how well students are learning to be active and effective seekers and evaluators of information.

Many academic libraries have gate counts that appear to be falling at the same time that they have a lessening use, though standard interfaces, of our increasing electronic resources. Use from outside the library building is rising (for one library, it is already at 75 percent). Students increasingly are bypassing library resources and going directly onto the World Wide Web. The standard measures for library excellence ignore most of these important changes. Local assessment methods must be developed to demonstrate real effectiveness to deans, provosts, and presidents.

Increasingly, college and university administrators focus on their relationships within and standing in consortia. Particular care should be taken to make sure that these figures are correct and that their interpretation is accurate. Institutions that are smaller or larger than their peers may be advantaged or disadvantaged apropos of certain measures. For instance, Penn State invariably fares poorly in the Committee on Institutional Cooperation on any measure done on a per-student basis. Our large number of students dilutes efforts and inevitably drives the university to the bottom of the comparator list.

Throughout recent years, library administrators have made much of the issue of past buying power. We continue to compare our current ability to purchase a core set of journals and books in the various disciplines with superior coverage in the past. The graphs are stunning in the clarity with which they indicate how much costs are rising and at the same time how much libraries' budgets are shrinking. Certainly, the diminishing ability to buy a respectable percentage of the total output of the scholarly communications system is a poster child story. Nevertheless, increasingly, the response from administrators and university planning committees is "so what?" Costs in many areas of higher education are rising rapidly. Library administrators need to begin thinking about how to supplement this cost disparity information with measures of effectiveness and lost effectiveness. One other caution in this area is that university presidents prefer to hear good news. To the extent that the serials pricing problem is not good news, information about it should be presented cautiously.

Equity

In "University Libraries: The 7-Per-Cent Solution," James Shapiro discussed the percentage of university budget as a measure of which institutions were supporting their libraries better.[3] Many library administrators have long seen this measure as a key one. Use of it as an assessment vehicle has declined for a number of reasons. One is that it often results in bad news for the administration. Another is that college and university budgets have become quite complex and academic officials will quickly argue that it is the way in which certain figures are being interpreted that is causing the poor result rather than the lack of support for the library.

Equity inside the institution is also difficult to assess. Recently, I compared the percentage of university budgets being spent to support academic programs at the different geographical locations of the university to the percentage of the libraries' materials budgets being spent there. Figures also were generated by the colleges at University Park to indicate what percentage was spent on that college's programs by the university and in the library materials budget. Several important factors were not reflected in this gross analysis. Most importantly, the relative cost of journals in the different disciplines was absent. Nevertheless, the figures did indicate a certain equity between the university's and the library's investments in each area. The most persistent result was that those colleges that had been rich and powerful in the past were the ones who are so now and their materials budgets reflect that political reality. A more impressive assessment project would have been to calculate what portion of student and faculty need is being met locally and what portion must rely on the access paradigm. Then some work could have been done on the level of satisfaction of those individuals.

Bragging rights

Administrators of all kinds enjoy bragging about the accomplishments of their institutions. The acquisition of new electronic resources has become a part of this rite of passage. Librarians should keep their administrators informed about where they are in the purchase of these products and if decisions are being made not to buy, rationales should be provided throughout the process. Some electronic resources were funded from foundations whose support is critical to many colleges and universities. The developers of these products have not been shy about using their powerful, high level connections with institutions of higher education to force librarians into decisions.

The only effective way that a library can counter such political maneuvers is to have a strong history of credible assessment projects that have measured the faculty and student reactions to these projects. Many students and some faculty are quite disappointed about the coverage in some of these projects.

Faculty

Faculty have equally complicated and sophisticated interests in library collections. Colleges and universities operate in a matrix environment with faculty having dual loyalty to their discipline and to their hiring institution. Discipline measures, standards, and contacts are used to determine the internal rewards of the academic institution—tenure, promotion, and merit. Faculty often identify more clearly with their disciplines and have more loyalty to them than they do to their hiring institutions.

Faculty need various supporting services from the library, many of which are beyond the provision of information, to support their research and teaching. They expect the library to be a showcase for their work. That includes buying and displaying their latest monograph and proceedings. Colleges and smaller universities often provide an annual reception to recognize the individuals and the work. Library participation in such events should be viewed as a fine opportunity for positive publicity. More difficult to handle diplomatically is the issue of a faculty member who edits a journal. Many expect the library to subscribe. Explaining to them either that serials monies are not available and/or that the journal does not match collecting parameters is a sophisticated diplomatic task. Most awkward of all would be to have to say that the journal's quality and reputation are not sufficient for its inclusion in the collection.

Many assessment studies indicate that faculty do not use libraries actively in their research. Research scientists in particular tend to rely on personal collections and on a network of contacts. More and more issues are being discussed electronically long before they appear in print. The real communication in science may be seen as being informal, but, of course, the system of print publication establishes precedence, ownership of ideas and concepts, and credit, which translates into tenure, promotion, and merit on the local campus. Nevertheless, because issues of prestige are involved, a library cannot be excused from collecting in subdisciplines where the university has strong and distinguished faculty. Whether these collections are used or not, they provide a testimony to the prestige of the discipline on campus. The most obvious examples of this revolve around branch libraries. Any assessment of the viability of a branch somehow must account for the status issues of the faculty in the discipline in order to be useful.

Faculty in the disciplines also need to understand how their scholarly communications designs affect the whole of academia. Librarians who can articulate the issues in this area should involve themselves with scholarly society leaders, information technology experts, and college and university administrators. Only through such broad conversations can libraries assume new roles for the future and cease the annual rite of serials cuts.

Thus, collection assessment to persuade faculty that changes are needed is a complex and sophisticated process. Some will be convinced by rising cost figures, cost-per-use data, use data, and alternative access modes. Others will object to them. These objections may take the form of arguments about the process for compiling the data and the meaning of the data or they may take the form of discounting the data process altogether. Many of these attacks arise from those issues described above; rational responses may not satisfy. In such instances, the whole issue may have to be resolved at a higher level in the organization. If the probability of such a result exists, serious consultation should occur before the assessment process begins. Even then, more than one university librarian has found him- or herself without administration support in processes such as those for closing a branch library.

Undergraduate Students

In decades past, student needs might not have been as highly regarded as they are today. The competition among institutions of higher education for students has placed some focus on appealing to what students want. Undergraduate and graduate students approach the library with a somewhat different point of view. The general needs of undergraduates fall into several categories.

Convenience

Convenience is a primary concern for the many undergraduates who may find Sunday night the appropriate time to begin a term paper due on Monday morning. As many students operate on an internal clock that differs from standard business hours, the advent of anytime, anyplace service via electronic systems is beneficial. Undergraduates find it convenient to use library resources remotely, and as much as 75 percent of use is already remote for some academic institutions. Some institutions are beginning to see a decline in statistics measuring the use of catalogs and databases. Library administrators believe that this use may have migrated into Web-based interfaces and directly onto the Web. Assessing the level and nature of remote use is a task of the greatest importance if libraries are to continue to meet undergraduate needs in a credible manner.

Generation X

Some characteristics of Generation X students are applicable here. They have a craving for stimulation because they have grown up in an age of media sound bites and infotainment. Variety is preferred over boring, routine, and monotonous activities, which tend to discourage Xers. Xers need personal contact. While they are culturally independent, they demand personal attention and feedback from teachers and librarians. They have a preference for concrete, specific information. Their preference is to have information service packaged in concise, laser-printed format that they can use at their convenience. They have a desire to learn leading-edge technology and to be associated with technological expertise.[4] The reasons they prefer electronic full-text resources to print ones are easy to see.

Glitz

Finally, undergraduates like their information resources to be glitzy. An environment of intensive marketing has shaped their tastes in a way that makes them greatly prefer the presentations on the World Wide Web. Because electronic information appears better to them and seems more up-to-date, they value it more than they value print information. Experts estimate that only 5 percent of the information on the World Wide Web is scholarly in nature, while perhaps as much as 95 percent of information in an academic library has been refereed through a discipline, edited by professional publishers, and selected by librarians.

This evolving situation provides a major challenge to librarians who must work with the teaching faculty to improve student work habits. While these student perceptions and desires exert a significant pull to bring more legitimate information onto the Web, faculty habits of establishing precedence for work and awarding credit for discovery and the entire structure of the existing promotion and tenure system seek to anchor scholarly communications in the print environment. In the area of student use of information resources, assessment must be used frequently, repeatedly, and effectively to measure what students are using, how that affects the quality of their work, and whether their overall learning experience is deteriorating.

Graduate Students

Many consider graduate students to be the most discriminating and serious users of the library. They have not yet developed strong personal libraries and networks of colleagues. Thus, they still depend on the library to be the primary source of materials for their papers and theses. Doctoral students, in particular, are actively engaged in becoming socialized to the discipline and how it carries on its communications. Librarians should look for opportunities to discuss this issue with them and to explain how the dysfunctions in the system have driven up the costs of journals, thereby reducing the amount of material available locally.

Graduate students often operate in the access environment. They work on narrow topics and traditionally have been required to conduct exhaustive literature searches. Quick, effective, and polite interlibrary loan is required for good service. Patron-initiated interlibrary loan, which is already available in many regions, helps graduate students. Those initiating such services will find graduate students to be a good group to use for assessment of effectiveness. Regular assessment exercises with graduate students to make sure their aggressive needs are being met are worthwhile. They are the future faculty.

Other Librarians

In those halcyon days of expansion, librarians were more attentive to building collections that were enviable to other librarians than they are today. Still, the ideal of a comprehensive collection exists and some strive for it. Subject librarians are relatively focused on meeting the needs of their primary discipline clientele. As such, they reflect the college and university administrators' requirements for national reputation, equity, and bragging rights. In many academic institutions, the division of the materials budget relies more heavily on a historical understanding of the powerful departments than on any other factor. While political power can never be discounted, some subject librarians have an excellent opportunity to use assessment tools that will show their programs have grown in size and prestige and are, therefore, worthy of greater support.

How to Do Assessment

When communication with key audiences requires assessment, the next step is selecting among the many methods available. This section discusses quantitative methods, qualitative ones, and benchmarking, which combines some aspects of both quantitative and qualitative methods.

Quantitative Methods

Quantitative methods to be discussed include system-generated statistics, questionnaires, and other traditional methods of collection assessment. Methods here are merely noted. Setting out to do a collection assessment by using one or more of these methods will require further research into library literature and the descriptive literature on the methods. Assessment is an expensive activity—effective assessment requires careful design, good collection methods, and cautious interpretation. Whenever possible, experts should be used to assist with the studies.

System-generated statistics
Most libraries rely on automated library systems for a variety of fairly static data—the number of additions to the collection in various areas and the circulation patterns of materials. Much can be learned from these figures; they are especially relevant when the assumption has been made that the library will operate in the access paradigm. Locally owned material should be material that is actively used when it is new because, in many fields, that is when it has its greatest value.

Many studies of newly developed electronic resources are now making much greater use of system-generated information. For instance, Carol Mandel, in studying the effectiveness of Columbia University's Online Books Evaluation Project, was able to measure several characteristics of the user population (where they were physically, their disciplines, and the length of time they spent on searching, using preliminary screens, and then accessing the text itself). The project combined statistics from the automated system with server statistics and user database information. Mandel supplemented that information with questionnaires that were delivered online, on-site, in classes, and by mail. The analysis was further enriched through the collection of information about costs. Qualitative methods, such as individual interviews and focus groups, provided a final set of information that allowed for a sophisticated assessment of user reactions to electronic monographs.[5]

This project is an exemplary one because of the amount of understanding that derives from the multiple methods of data collection and the strong interpretation of results. All data, by whatever method they are collected, must be interpreted to be understood. Data without understanding are useless. Understanding then requires relating data to service objectives and changing them accordingly.

Speaking at the Association of Research Libraries Monographs conference, Clifford Lynch noted that studies such as the Columbia Online Books Evaluation Project will not have a long shelf life because the needs and characteristics of users of electronic information will be changing rapidly. Products themselves are changing and the interfaces to them are critically important to their effectiveness with students and faculty.[6] Short lifespan of assessment work is a new factor in collection assessment and one of the most important points of this chapter. To be effective, assessment work must be done well and redone frequently.

Lynch also defined a different emphasis for collections people in the future. In an age of information overload, identifying what is new and how to find it will be a critical library task. Attention must be brought to bear on electronic collections and resources worthy of attention, and in many ways that is a new duty for collections officers.

Questionnaires

Questionnaires continue to be an effective method for gathering opinion data from students and faculty. They are not, however, as easy as they appear to create, administer, and interpret. Questionnaires can be used at two levels—at the research level, where the instrument has been fully tested, the administration has been appropriately randomized, and the interpretation can be generalized. They also can be used at the continuous quality improvement or total quality management level, where the results will not be generalizable but will be helpful in redefining local services. The audience should determine which level will be required. Nevertheless, any kind of questionnaire, no matter how casual, must ask the right questions in the right way. Design is critical and expert advice should be sought in that process. Many colleges and universities have departments whose function is to advise in these areas. If that service is not available, campus colleagues still may be willing to offer assistance. In addition, many major divisions of the American Library Association have statistics and research committees who help members with these issues.

Other traditional methods of collection analysis

Among the different branches of librarianship, collections officers have been in the forefront of developing methods for assessing the effectiveness of their work. In the same way that system-generated statistics and questionnaires continue to be effective means of gathering data for assessment, many other methods are valid. These include

- compiling statistics,
- checking lists,
- direct observation of collections,
- applying standards,
- user surveys,
- availability and accessibility measures,
- citation analysis,
- circulation statistics,
- measuring in-library use, and
- periodical use study

Blaine Hall's *Collection Assessment Manual for College and University Libraries* continues to be a rich resource for understanding the applicability of these methods.[7]

Qualitative Methods

Qualitative methods have been less extensively used for collection assessment than quantitative ones. In the humanities and social sciences in general, qualitative methods are assuming new stature. Because they allow understanding of some reasons behind actions and because they can guide services toward satisfying student and faculty needs more clearly, they are gaining more widespread use and credibility in librarianship. Methods discussed below include focus groups, interviews, and unobtrusive observation.

A focus group is a formal gathering of a group of students and faculty to discuss a set of questions. Like questionnaires, focus groups appear to be simpler than they are. The design of the questions, the configuration of the room, the group of attendees, the moderator, the recording device, and techniques for handling awkward occurrences all require a high level of sophistication. The literature and campus or professional experts should be consulted to design this exercise. Nevertheless, the results of focus groups can be extremely useful in redesigning services and they seem to have good credibility on campuses as a way of determining student needs.

Clearly, when librarians have coffee with discipline faculty to discuss support for the subject area, those librarians are doing informal interviews. If the results of such informal interviews are regularly recorded and aggregated and if the interviews cover multiple individuals with multiple points of view, then these data can be quite useful. More formal interviews, with structured lists of questions and established times and interviewees, can also be a rich source of information. Interviews provide a good vehicle for deciding which problems might be presented to focus groups. As with questionnaires, better designs will yield better results, and experts and the literature should be consulted.

With many faculty and administrators, unobtrusive observation has the highest credibility of any. In librarianship, this method is seldom used for a number of reasons. Library faculty and staff members are extremely hostile to being observed either by a person or by a video camera. The results presented in the premier work in this area, Peter Hernon and Chuck McClure's book on government documents, have further entrenched the library community against this method.[8] Yet librarians know very little about how students use information resources. As the provision of information changes more and more rapidly, the need to understand the students' actions and thinking will increase. This excellent method should not be overlooked.

Benchmarking

Benchmarking is a relatively new addition to the library assessment portfolio. Briefly, benchmarking is the search for best practices. It allows an individual library to identify a problem, search out another library that seems to be doing the best job with it, and then identify the process that gives the superior result. For instance, Carol Mandel's work on the Columbia Online Books Evaluation Project currently represents a best practice in the field of assessing the effectiveness of an electronic resource. Benchmarking comparisons might be made through reading the Website, hearing a talk about it, reading an article on it, or interviewing Mandel and others at Columbia.

Quantitative studies often will provide a basis for benchmarks with other libraries. If a library identifies an area in which its statistics are not as good as those of other libraries, that is an area for further exploration through benchmarking. Benchmarking involves the development of flow charts, various contacts with customers, and, in the end, interviews with the best practitioner.

In industry, some firms publish the best practices in certain standard operations that may exist in many different kinds of companies. The creation of such a series of best practices for library services and collections would be a most worthwhile enterprise. Such a work could include results, costs, processes, and discussions of particular challenges in conceiving and maintaining the standard. Because library materials go out of date so quickly, older collections methods of comparing against standard lists such as *Books for College Libraries* have lost some of their effectiveness. A benchmarking approach to this problem might be to gain permission to review current acquisitions in areas of interest and to discuss the methods the best practitioner uses for making selections. Such benchmarking offers a quick road to substantive improvement.[9]

Conclusions

Libraries should undertake more assessment. The assessments undertaken should be targeted to the concerns and expectations of specific audiences— college and university administrators, faculty, students, and other librarians. An expanding number of assessment methods, including quantitative methods, qualitative ones, and benchmarking, are applicable to collection assessment projects. The results of assessment studies are much more limited in their applicability than they were formerly. The dynamics of changing library users, electronic information, and delivery systems require frequent reassessments. Individuals who use assessment to tailor their collections to the documented needs of students and faculty will be building active, dynamic, and satisfying collections.

Notes

1. Ronald F. Dow, "Assessment in an Era of Accountability," *Journal of Academic Librarianship* 24, no. 3 (May 1998): 197–99.
2. See, for example: Ross Atkinson, "Access, Ownership, and the Future of Collection Development," in *Collection Management and Development: Issues in an Electronic Era,* ed. Peggy Johnson and Bonnie MacEwan (Chicago: American Library Association, 1994), 92–119 and his "Acquisitions Librarian as Change Agent in the Transition to the Electronic Library," *Library Resources & Technical Services* 36 (January 1992): 11–15.
3. James Shapiro, "University Libraries: The 7-Per-Cent Solution," *Chronicle of Higher Education* (December 12, 1997), B 4–5.
4. David Cannon, "Generation X: The Way They Do the Things They Do," *Journal of Career Planning and Employment* 51 (1991): 34–38; Catherine A. Lee, "The Changing Face of the College Student: The Impact of Generation X on Reference and Instructional Services," in *The Changing Face of Reference,* ed. Lynne M. Stuart and Dena Holiman Hutto (Greenwich, Conn.: JAI Press, 1996), 107–18.
5. Descriptions of the Columbia University Online Books Evaluation Project can be found on the Columbia Libraries Website: http://www.columbia.edu/cu/libraries/ digital/texts/about.html and in "Online Books at Columbia: Measurement and Early Results on Use, Satisfaction, and Effect: Interim Report of the Andrew W. Mellon

Foundation-Funded Columbia University Online Books Evaluation Project," by Mary Summerfield, Carol A. Mandel, and Paul Kantor (paper presented at the Scholarly Communication and Technology Conference, Emory University, Atlanta, Ga., April 24–25, 1997), http://www.arl.org/scomm/scat/summerfield.ind.html.

6. Clifford Lynch, "What Will a Monograph Look Like in a Digital Library?" (Paper presented at the conference The Specialized Scholarly Monograph in Crisis or How Can I Get Tenure If You Won't Publish My Book?, Washington, D.C., September 11–12, 1997).

7. Blaine H. Hall, *Collection Assessment Manual for College and University Libraries* (Phoenix: Oryx, 1985).

8. Peter Hernon and Charles R. McClure, *Improving the Quality of Reference Service for Government Publications* (Chicago: American Library Association, 1983).

9. Gloriana St. Clair, "Restructuring and Benchmarking: Partners for Change," in *Restructuring Academic Libraries: Organization Development in the Wake of Technology Change,* ed. Charles A. Schwartz, ACRL Publications in Librarianship, no. 49 (Chicago: American Library Association, 1997), 200–212.

7

Libraries: The Changing Political and Economic Environment

Kenneth E. Dowlin

The phrase "virtually yours" is a catchy one. It is something that could be scored by Nat King Cole for one of his dreamy songs. Actually, he would probably do it for his daughter, Natalie, who is more hip. Another phrase I think of is one I heard from Margaret Knox Goggin, retired Dean of the Denver University School of Library and Information Science. In her Isabel Nichol Lecture at the school, she quoted John Naisbitt on times being in dramatic change. Goggin spoke about the fact that libraries are in "a time of parentheses."[1] That is, we are not what we were and we are not what we will be. As I think of the future of libraries, I often think of that phrase. I am sure that Naisbitt and Goggin both were making the point that the time was unusual. It was interesting when I heard it in 1984. Even years later it is still relevant. We have been in a time of parentheses for decades and it will continue for even more decades. Change is now the norm. While it is relatively easy to understand where we have been and possible to articulate where we are now, it is very difficult to predict where we are going. In order to predict the future, one must know the past. My interest and studies in history lead me take a long-term view and, when considering societal change, I envision the future by looking backward.

I feel qualified to comment on the future because of my thirty-five years in the library business, and my expertise in using information technology to develop and enhance libraries and their services. I am typecast as a techno-librarian because of my pioneering work in library information technology and publications. In 1984 in *The Electronic Library: The Promise and the Process,* I proposed that the Electronic Library that was emerging would have four characteristics:

> management of resources with a computer,

> ability to link the information provider with the information seeker via electronic channels,

> ability for staff to intervene in the electronic transaction when requested by the information seeker,

> ability to store, organize, and transmit information to the information seeker via electronic channels.[2]

I learned from my experience in building the new San Francisco main library that one of the challenges in a project of that size, which took over eight years to complete, is to plan for the use of the technology that changes generations every eighteen months. Yet the inclusion of current information and communication technology was critical in order to build one of the first large twenty-first-century libraries in the world. It may be one of the last, due to the ignorant press reports about local controversies.

This challenge can be summed up in a statement by Walter Gretzky, Wayne Gretzky's father. His advice, "Skate to where the puck's going to be, not where it has been. Anticipate. Anticipate," should be heeded by all librarians.

The most central technological element driving the shape of our future is the Internet. In a very short period, even in an environment that is accustomed to rapid change, the Internet has become a

- new medium that has the ability to surpass all other media in scale,
- cultural phenomenon that has not seen this much attention since the emergence of television,
- tool for connecting the world,
- great equalizer for access to the libraries of the world.

It is global, extremely dynamic, and expanding by the second. Paul Evan Peters characterized the Internet as a "Cloud of Users."[3] I agreed with him at first, but now I feel that the Internet is not just an unorganized mass of stuff. The companies and institutions that are creating navigation tools for the Internet are providing the organization needed for the virtual library. The virtual library is here now.

At the end of the nineteenth century and the early twentieth century, libraries were mostly built as warehouses for storing scarce books for shared use by the community. The use of the library was available only to the visitors of the buildings. Later in the twentieth century, the library began reaching out to the community through branch buildings, bookmobile units, deposit stations, and communication technology such as the telephone. At the same time, the library incorporated new formats into the collections as they were developed. Magazines, serials, microforms, sound media, and video media augmented the book. The most recent additions are the computer and networked resources.

Whereas the role of the nineteenth-century library was mostly to provide shared on-site access to the common collection of books, the new technologies and formats allowed new roles. These roles included being the

- repository of knowledge;
- institution for access to information, knowledge, learning, and the joys of reading;
- center for engaging people in reading and learning;
- center for creating and maintaining community archives;
- resource for local governments or nonprofit institutions;
- community center for research;
- center for community information and referral;
- center for community based adult literacy programs.

The use of electronic information technology has accelerated the basic paradigm shift from the library oriented to the book and the user's visits to service provided throughout the community (to the home, office, or school), regardless of location and original format. Because moving the services of the library onto the Internet has only a marginal cost, we are now creating the fastest growing library in history. In the twenty-first century, the legacy for libraries will move from that of Andrew Carnegie to that of Bill Gates. The magnitude of this paradigm shift can be best described by going "Back to the Future."

Peter Lyman compares today's impact of the Internet to the one when technology for facsimile communication became a medium for political exiles, particularly those from behind the Iron Curtain.[4] That observation caused me to recall that during the time of the massacre of Tiananmen Square in China, some of the first communication of the events as they unfolded was from Beijing to the fax machine at the San Francisco Public Library. One of the young people on-site had been an employee at the library and had the fax telephone number. The library staff shared the information with the national wire services, thus becoming the window into a mist of censorship for the world at large. Lyman states that the Internet gives voice to social movements with no political voice, enabling those who feel isolated locally to reach out and gain a sense of community or solidarity on a national or global scale. A more sweeping observation comes from Carla Hesse, who points out the similarity between the paradigm shift in publishing at the end of the eighteenth century and changes at the end of the twentieth century. Hesse views the similarities of the experimentation with microtechnologies as a means of putting the power of publication into the hands of every individual citizen as quite parallel even though the events are three hundred years apart. The desirable outcome in the views of Condorcet was to bring all of France into a dialogue with itself.

Unfortunately, the French Revolution intervened and the change was not completed fully. It did, however, lead to the recognition of intellectual property, the notion of the right-bearing and accountable individual author, the value of democratic access to useful knowledge, and faith in free market competition as the most effective mechanism of public exchange. Unfortunately, the new government returned to the habits of the former crown and reinstituted censorship, which took hundreds of years to repeal.[5] When we look back on the late twentieth century, how will we describe the changes in communication technology?

Variables That Impact the Future

In projecting ahead to the next millennium, I believe that the following ten factors will have the biggest impact on the specifics and direction of the paradigm shift for libraries.

The Next Generation

The children of today will be adults who are comfortable with the new technology. In fact, they will expect their institutions and communities to provide the electronic tools as a part of the environment. Schools, public libraries, and other institutions are teaching very young children to use computers and networking. The adeptness of small children with video games is embarrassing to most of my generation. My niece's daughter of ten was able to defeat me easily in video games. For perhaps the first time in history, the elders are forced to learn from the children. I believe that the children's techno-literacy will force libraries to cope with the new technology whether they want to or not. The libraries that lead in service-oriented information technology implementation will thrive. The others may become irrelevant to their community or, at best, marginal.

Demographics

Perhaps more than at any other time in recent history, entire populations are on the move. This global phenomenon is increasing diversity in communities all over the world and thus creating new challenges to existing communities. The need for shared values in communities is becoming critical. John Gardner contends that creating, enhancing, or preserving the community is one of the most important social needs of our time.[6] Migrations are putting pressures on traditional communities from the new populations and their increasing cultural diversity. Libraries have a significant opportunity for leadership in their community if they become institutions that create an overarching sense of the whole community while simultaneously celebrating our diverse cultural heritages.

Borders, Barnes & Noble, and Crown

Bookstores have changed in major ways. The megastores are providing many of the services that were considered the province of the public library. For example, a warm, inviting place with thousands of titles to peruse is now available in most cities at these stores. Their emphasis on customer service and amenities goes beyond what was the norm for public libraries. Their ability to use sophisticated marketing tools ensures that they are in the forefront of the public's attention. They may capture the population that has been the mainstay of the library market—the educated and family-oriented middle class. The tradition of an author reading at the library is dwindling as the marketing experts tie book promotion to commercial enterprises such as bookstores.

Amazon.com

There is a new actor on the book business front because of the Internet. Amazon.com claims to be the largest bookstore on the planet. I am very impressed with their level of service, communication, and convenience. I now use them for my book shopping needs. After attempting to find a Japanese cookbook and a Scandinavian travel book for my wife at the local branch of the public library and then the bookstore and failing at both, I turned to the Internet and found both at Amazon.com. The books arrived in two days and I was very satisfied with the timeliness. The provision of reviews by standard sources, the readers, and even the author enhances the aura of the company being a friendly, helpful place. Their interactive, immediate response to orders fosters a high level of trust in the company. Some of the historic mainline publishers and megastores are now using the Internet. Their aggregate impact on the traditional users of libraries and small bookstores is significant.

University Presidents, Bean Counters, and Governors

The future of libraries in the public sector is determined through politics. That is the American way and I know of no better system for collective decision making. The decisions to create the Virtual Library or the Virtual University will be made by the funders and politicians. The president of the University of California and the State Librarian of California recently announced the initiation of the Virtual Library of California. The plans for the library at the newest campus of the University of California, Monterey Bay, were heavily weighted against building a traditional library. The governors of most of the states in the West have announced plans to create a Virtual University that would serve higher education needs in a wide geographic area. The School of Library and Information Science at San Jose State University is working on the creation of the Virtual Library School to deliver instruction throughout the state of California, perhaps beyond. The important point for us to understand about all these announcements is that while "virtual" institutions are touted as a way to increase efficiency and effectiveness of the programs, the real reason that the politicians like them is they believe virtual libraries will save money over the traditional methods of providing library service. Nothing motivates politicians more than the thought that they can save money, except the possibility that they can get reelected.

The Library Paradox

One issue surfacing in the popular press and literary magazines is the worry that the computer will somehow taint libraries, that the books will all be discarded and the librarians put out to pasture. Library leaders clearly face a dilemma of how to incorporate the tools of the information age so clearly desired by their communities and do it in a way that the support of the historic user is not lost. The literary and even the popular press have gone overboard in their nostalgic portrayal of the library as a quiet, literary mausoleum. An author in a recent edition of a new online magazine, *Salon,* has stereotyped librarians as being committed to the principle that digital content will replace all the books. I have no idea how she arrived at the conclusion but, reading the article, it is obvious that having computer terminals for the OPAC in the entrance of the library is seen as more than just a catalog. They are viewed as only the tip of the iceberg. And, there must be a conspiracy somewhere.

Publishing

The publishing business is undergoing a far-reaching change. Few family-owned book publishers remain. Media conglomerates with little interest beyond the bottom line have gobbled up the firms that were committed to quality for the readers and libraries. Publishing is now part of an industry focusing on blockbuster sales that rely on media stars, sports figures, politicians, and courtrooms. As an industry, print publishing now ranks fourth behind television, cinema, and even video games. The increasing costs of serial publications and the demand for new media have forced libraries to reduce the number of monograph purchases. As a result, small presses and marginally profitable titles are facing very difficult times. The electronic technology now available for scholarly communications well may provide the access and distribution mechanism that will bypass all the traditional publishers. The High-Wire Press at Stanford University demonstrates that the future of scholarly communications is being created now.

The Cult of the Book

The kamikaze tactics of fanatic devotees of the book feed on the fears of many people concerning change. Those who clutch to the ideal that the book is the only appropriate technology for the library need little encouragement to insist that the library must dig in its heels. This environment creates a contentious situation in many communities. The contention is blown totally out of proportion by the press. In some cases, tremendous time and effort must be expended to counter harm to the institution. The decision that the library would include other formats was made when the first magazine was purchased and reinforced with the purchase of microforms, videos, and other formats.

Libraries Do Change

Libraries have not only changed over the last century, they often have been pioneers. Many libraries were using barcodes before the grocery stores. Librarians have led all other professions in networking. We developed the interlibrary loan code in the 1930s through ALA. Cooperative indexing and cataloging have been the norm for many decades. Self-checkout of materials is becoming common in many libraries. In Europe, the appearance of robots for sorting and shelving books is an interesting development. Our past successes in change predict success in the future.

Change Means Opportunities

A time of changes means the opportunity to increase shared resources and thus save physical space and money on the purchase of expensive items. The new information technology has reduced dramatically the time lag for the acquisition and handling of books and other collection items. Since our consumers are now conditioned by the advertising industry to demand instant gratification, the time frames of the old interlibrary loan days are no longer acceptable to the library users. I was impressed thirty years ago by the concept that books have a time value. The longer time necessary to produce a book for a user, the less value the book has. The time lines that libraries previously viewed as the norm are no longer acceptable. On-demand delivery of documents may be the budget savior for many libraries not only by allowing decreased subscription budgets, but also by putting a lid on the recent uncontrollable cost increases. Document delivery service also can mitigate increases in labor costs. The Internet has erased geographic barriers that surrounded libraries all over the world. Any library that mounts a Website and provides information has just added their library to the global village. The potential user base is not only expanding geographically. It now also reaches the techno snobs who have viewed the traditional library as passé.

Over time, the costs of equipment and telecommunication may shift from the library to the user. If libraries are set up for laptop computers, access through the Internet, or dial-up ports, the user will assume the cost of the hardware, maintenance, and soft costs such as paper and printer toner. While this requires technological change outside libraries, the payoff for libraries could be enormous.

Technology allows the library to expand existing roles and add new roles with only a marginal cost. Public libraries could become the community communications and information center. The archiving of electronic community information is barely developed and mostly neglected. In fact, the community information and referral function assumed by many public libraries starting in the 1970s probably will flow back to the agencies with the statutory or contractual responsibility, since the Internet allows each agency a low-cost mechanism for acquiring, organizing, and delivering this information. Perhaps now the library should focus more on the archiving of the information for historical purposes than in its direct provision. The global village library is now less a technology issue than one of organization. Roles and responsibilities to the community and to the global village need to be developed, articulated, and broadcast for all to use for making decisions about access. Common terminology and structure need to be developed that will allow automatic indexers and locators to identify accurately the library sites and resources available on those sites. Few question that libraries will be in the business of technology training and support for their staff and users. The public views libraries as institutions that will provide a safety net for access to information technology for general citizens. Interest in the Virtual University and distance education brings significant new opportunities for recasting university libraries. Stanford University has merged the programs of the University Library and the scholarly communication program. What will emerge will be a phenomenon that I call the "Knowledge Bridge"—a mechanism to bridge the gap between the knowledge industry, such as universities and publishers, and the communication industry, such as TV and other popular media. The ultimate development is the rise of the library as a community icon for information and knowledge access. While being an icon is a significant rise in stature, it is also a large burden (I witnessed the result of such an elevation of stature in San Francisco and can speak to both the stature and burden).

We are experiencing a paradigm shift in libraries. Service is moving from finding the right book for the right person at the right time to connecting the right data information or knowledge to the right person at the right time.

Even with the tremendous communication capability brought to the individual by the information technology revolution, libraries still will be important to their communities. They bring stability, public subsidy, validation of sources, authentication of publishers, continuity, community, and a sense of geography even in the virtual world. Librarians bring added value to the content as well as their values of service, intellectual freedom, and respect for the privacy of the individual user.

Change Means Challenges

There must be the definition, acceptance, and articulation of roles and responsibilities of local libraries for the global audience. Since the commercial sector rapidly is undertaking many of the functions traditionally done by libraries, the profession of librarianship must keep developing new roles and services. The navigation and location aides such as Yahoo, Lycos, Alta Vista, HotBot, and others have taken over the task of cataloging the electronic resources on the Internet. I used to call the Internet the largest version of "Dungeons & Dragons" in history. That is no longer the case. The process of making the links from traditional access mechanisms, such as catalogs, to the source information has become very simple. It is easy to imbed URLs in MARC records.

I am concerned that librarians will face the fates of travel agents, bank tellers, stockbrokers, and switchboard operators, even though changes are being made very rapidly in the field of librarianship. A profession that was viewed as among the least stressful in the 1980s has become one of stress in the 1990s. Librarians must understand their roles will change from a service orientation to one of management—managing collections, paraprofessionals, technicians, volunteers, and a variety of technologies. Peter Young contends that we are in a period of "postmodern librarianship."[7] Klaus-Dieter Lehmann provides an illuminating look at the issues around archiving for librarians.[8] Reconciling the future users with the traditional users will be daunting. Most libraries are scrambling to find the funds through both developing new funds and shifting existing budgets. All potential funding sources are being considered, including institutional, grants, private funds, and those generated by sharing costs. The global nature of the Internet will aggravate the existing gap between the funding and need. The divergence between the users and the funders is a sleeping time bomb.

An entirely new challenge for library directors is created by the drive for additional funds to provide new programs. The education of stakeholders in the sources of funds is critical for the success of an institution. The San Francisco Public Library during my tenure as City Librarian was one of the most successful libraries in history in increasing dollars for library development and operation. The citizens of San Francisco committed nearly $600 million to the library through tax measures, charter amendments, and private donations. Yet most of the users, the staff, and the critics seldom saw a connection between the quality and breadth of library services and the ability to raise money. The audit concluded in the spring of 1997 states emphatically that "[the library must] provide basic financial literacy training for staff at all levels so that they are knowledgeable about what drives the Library's revenue and expenses and what they can do to positively affect overall financial performance. . . . This should be a major focus of staff training efforts in the next year."

Perhaps there needs to be some transformation of library associations. Learned, in *The American Public Library and the Diffusion of Knowledge,* stated in 1924 that "ALA . . . [could] become supremely useful . . . by supplying an intelligent agency for organizing their printed materials."[9] Ken Carpenter states that this never happened.[10] In fact, the central organizing entities for library collections in the United States have been the Library of Congress and OCLC, not the professional association.

Another challenge is the development and support of leaders who dare to transform the library in preparation for the twenty-first century. Of the library directors who created or oversaw the building of major new main libraries in the United States in the last decade, there are only two who remain as directors more than a year after the project completion. The president of Brazil's Biblioteca Nacional led the planning for the transformation of public library service in Brazil only to lose his job over a political battle. The director of the Maalmo, Sweden, Public Library suffered the same fate.

The Future

Umberto Eco declares that the model for the future of libraries in the electronic information world may be the Rube Goldberg model.[11] Maybe the song won't be from the repertory of Nat King Cole. It might be from Frank Sinatra: "Do it my way." I am optimistic about our profession's ability to change. With organization, we can move ahead for the collective good. Gary Larson portrays in one of his famous Far Side cartoons a pile of horses and deputies outside the sheriff's office as he says, "And you just threw everything together? . . . Matthews, a posse is something you have to organize." I think that if we develop Virtual Library Schools for entry-level education for the profession, schools that can provide life-long learning programs for librarians, and create programs to educate "architects" of virtual libraries, we will thrive in the twenty-first century.

The Magic of Libraries Comes from the Connections

Cathy Simon, one of the architects for the SFPL main library, is quoted in *The Future of the Book* as "conceiving of the new library as exemplifying an architecture of motion—a kinetic architecture—comprised, weblike, of nodes, intersections, and passages. It is not volumes delimited by walls."[12] Carla Hesse states, "[the library] in San Francisco [is] a reprisal of the cultural mission of civic humanism carried forward from the Renaissance Italian city-states to the postmodernist Pacific Rim."[13] I see the new library as being *the* intersection of words, information, knowledge, ideas and minds.

Notes

1. Margaret Knox Goggin, "Living in the Time of the Parentheses" (Paper delivered as an Isabel Nichol Lecture at the University of Denver, Colorado, 1984).
2. Kenneth E. Dowlin, *The Electronic Library: The Promise and the Process* (New York: Neal-Schuman, 1984), 33.
3. Paul Evan Peters, various speeches.
4. Peter Lyman, "What Is a Digital Library?: Technology, Intellectual Property, and the Public Interest," *Daedalus* (fall 1996): 19.
5. Carla Hesse, "Books in Time," in *The Future of the Book,* ed. Goeffrey Nunberg (Berkeley: University of California Press, 1996), 24–26.
6. John W. Gardner, *Building Community* (Palo Alto, Calif.: Leadership Studies Program of the Independent Sector, 1991), 5.
7. Peter Young, "Librarianship: A Changing Profession," *Daedalus* (fall 1996): 119.
8. Klaus-Dieter Lehmann, "Making the Transitory Permanent: The Intellectual Heritage in a Digitized World of Knowledge," *Daedalus* 125 (fall 1996): 307–29.
9. Kenneth E. Carpenter, "A Library Historian Looks at Librarianship," *Daedalus* 125 (fall 1996): 79.
10. Ibid., 89.
11. Umberto Eco, "Afterword," in *The Future of the Book,* ed. Geoffrey Nunberg (Berkeley: University of California Press, 1996), 306.
12. Hesse, "Books in Time," 30.
13. Ibid., 29.

PART III

Understanding "Digital" Libraries: Practical Implications

8

Today and Tomorrow: What the Digital Library Really Means for Collections and Services

Clifford Lynch

This chapter will take a hard and realistic look at some of the ramifications of digital information for library services, collections, and strategies. I used the phrase "digital library" in the title because I want to begin with this idea as a way of setting a context for the broader discussion that follows.

Digital Library

The phrase "digital library" is very fashionable these days. Everyone seems to be building a digital library. Not just libraries, but an amazing number of other institutions, organizations, and random individuals are building what they are calling digital libraries. It would be useful to explore what this term "digital library" really means to most people, because it is a problematic term to me. On one hand, it has an oxymoronic feel; on the other, it resonates with me, and I think with many other people, as a way of capturing how technology is really transforming not just libraries, but many profound social and cultural structures that are linked to institutions like libraries—for example, the acts of authorship and publication.

This paper is an edited transcription of the presentation Clifford Lynch gave at the Virtually Yours Institute.

One view of digital libraries that may be disconcerting to the "traditional" library community is that they are *information manipulation and use system environments*. (The adjective "traditional" is used only to distinguish between existing libraries that are trying to come to grips with the digital transformation, as opposed to all the other groups that are now positioning themselves as builders of digital libraries but that stand outside the historic institutional library traditions of selection, organization, access, and preservation.)

Many of the NASA/ARPA/NSF-funded digital library projects convey this perspective. These projects are designed for information users working in specific data-intensive environments. They are designed for people working with, for example, geospatial data or environmental data and related materials, who want to operate in a data-immersive environment.

When one looks at the computer science research world's view of digital libraries—as expressed by some of their systems—one sees no clear line between the library that is a storage place and active systems that facilitate communication and collaboration among researchers (e.g., control of experimental apparatus and sensor systems, data analysis environments, and authoring or annotation environments). The separation between readers and authors has become murky in some of these systems. One certainly does not get the sense they are thinking in terms of information that will persist for hundreds of years and of authors who will create works that will reach, and be reexamined by, many generations of future readers. There is a very strong focus on supporting current research activities. There is an important, although uncomfortable, message here for libraries as they think about how to draw the boundaries around their services in the digital environment. I will return to this issue several times in this chapter.

Before the computer scientists hijacked the term "digital library," many of us were really thinking more about "digital collections." We were thinking about libraries as we understand them today—extending their collections to encompass substantial amounts of digital materials, making use of information systems to provide access to them, and providing a coherence of access between their digital materials and their printed materials. People from the traditional library community look at the "digital library" and use that term as shorthand for any library that includes in its collection large amounts of digital material. They continue to see maintaining this coherence of access and coverage across collections, be they print or electronic, as an important goal.

None of us look forward to continuing and expanding the dichotomy we have historically constructed between books and journals to one in which you look one place for digital material, another place for printed monograph material, and yet another for journals. The problem is compounded by not being sure where to go depending on whether the journals are electronic or print. The trend and the objective over the last decade have been to provide greater coherence among collections previously treated disparately. If one looks at the evolution of the online catalog into complex systems that encompass large amounts of abstract and indexing information (and the University of California's Melvyl system is a good example here), one can see a road map that leads to convergence and greater coherence. There are some very powerful forces—market forces, in particular—that profoundly threaten our movement toward that coherence.

Redefining Library Service

Having provided some context about the term "digital library," I will now feel free to abuse it as shorthand for "digital collections in the libraries." Let me suggest some issues to help us redefine library services and shape the evolution of an environment increasingly characterized by digital information and the systems required to access and coordinate that digital information. Thinking about these boundaries is difficult and makes many uneasy, because we really do not want to have any limits. Librarians want to do everything, even as the resources get tighter and tighter. We get this queasy feeling that we should be doing an infinite number of things, even though our expertise and our resources are so limited in the face of an infinite agenda of service demands. Somehow we have to set priorities.

Data Sets

One issue we need to consider is what I call data sets. This is digital content that you do not read. You may render it or manipulate it with the aid of computer programs, but it is clearly not just some pile of paper that someone has transferred to digital form. There are a few classic examples. Many libraries have struggled with what to do with census data. There is no question that this information is a fundamental part of the primary research material for a wide range of scholarship. Geospatial data, digital maps, remote sensing information, and molecular biology databases are important and will be on any short list of working scholars' resource requirements in the relevant disciplines. No one would suggest this is fringe or optional material.

These data have some key characteristics that make a computer essential for its use. Most of what people want to do with it is computation-intensive. Contrast this kind of resource to an electronic journal. While you need a video monitor to read the electronic journal, reading is not an computation-intensive act. Most libraries easily can afford to buy all the computer power needed to enable large numbers of people to read this electronic information on a screen, but when you talk to people about geospatial and census data, you hear terms like "super computer." Most libraries do not have budgets for super computers.

Given the other pressures on their budgets, most probably are not eager to set up a budget line and have demand for super computer cycles compete against the latest round of journal price increases, but using these data requires computation. Where is the computation going to happen? Who's going to provide it? How does the library as perhaps manager or repository of these data relate to those computational resources?

This is a difficult boundary question right now. How much computation is acceptable inside the libraries' core systems and how much is the library purely an information warehouse or repository that feeds computation going on elsewhere? As we see more and more data becoming essential to more and more scholarly pursuits, this will become an increasingly critical issue. It is easy to think that this problem is limited purely to the sciences and social sciences. Don't believe it. A whole new discipline of computational humanism, usually lumped under the phrase "computing in the humanities," is developing. These folks are generating a lot of data. Think about all of the marked-up manuscripts and other texts being created now that the Text Encoding Initiative standards are in place. Consider computational linguistics, computation-intensive studies, or word use patterns and statistics and how they change across manuscripts. This is serious computation, too. Most libraries are fairly comfortable with the notion that text-encoded, marked-up manuscripts are a reasonable part of their collection. Having said that, what service framework do they need? What do you do with them?

Let me raise another point about this computation-intensive information. Suppose that computing becomes so cheap that it is not an issue. (I don't believe it is going to get that cheap, because every time computational capacity doubles, people think of more things to do with it, resulting in a perpetual pushing of the limits of feasible computation.) Who is going to teach people about what data sets there are, how to use them, and how they relate to these tools? I don't think this will be purely a library function. Certainly, I do not anticipate large numbers of librarians having second careers as instructors in statistical software or image manipulation software.

Yet it is clear that libraries are going to have a piece of the action. This is a new collaboration that will grow in the next decade between computer support people and faculty and librarians in a much more profound way. In some universities, I already am seeing computer lab support within the individual departments or schools, often in partnership with the library. It is increasingly integrated in the curriculum, particularly at the graduate level, rather than confined to a centralized university-wide computer lab system. The whole complex of issues around data sets is one situation where the boundaries are becoming very blurry and the stakes are very, very high.

Electronic Journals

Let me turn to another set of issues and another set of environmental factors that may affect service priorities—the transition of the printed journals to the electronic environment. Something very significant has happened in the last twelve to eighteen months. Much of the publishing industry has moved beyond experimental mode. We have seen a decade of interesting experiments and collaborations, looking at issues of translating journals into electronic form, how they'll be used, and what problems will arise. This year we have seen many of the major publishers, particularly in the scientific, technical, and medical areas, make commitments to bring up all or significant parts of their product line as standard commercial ventures that can be licensed on reasonably short time frames. What is fascinating is that about the time the publishers' mindset changed, the business model also changed.

Consider, for instance, most of the experiments in the early nineties: the Elsevier/Tulip Project, work with the American Chemical Society at Cornell, and the core project for the collaboration between the IEEE (Institute of Electrical and Electronics Engineers), the IEE (Institute of Electrical Engineers), and the University of California. What characterized all those projects is that libraries got the data and the material was mounted locally. This presented serious problems. Everybody thinks it is easy until they try it. Talk to any of the participants in the Tulip Project who figured casually at the beginning of the project, "Oh, we'll have this up in a few months; it's just bitmap images; this can't be very complicated, can it?" A year later they were still trying to fight their way through some of the implementation problems. People considered the experiments and then thought about scaling up and realized that it was not viable. Almost every one of the implementations for those experiments was custom software. Most commercial local library systems do not have facilities to import half a terabyte of bitmap images as a production input stream, process it, link it to the appropriate abstracting and indexing databases, and make it available for patron use on an ongoing basis. Doing this for several hundred publishers in parallel is almost unthinkable, so the publishers moved to a model where they are network-based information service providers, either directly or by subcontracting with a private service bureau or an aggregator. Elsevier, Springer, and Academic Press have put up Websites with their material. At some level, this is a relief for libraries. They can move forward into the world of largely electronic journals and bypass their local systems' inability to mount the material and their budgetary inability to make the necessary investments to develop or create local systems that can allow them to mount the material.

With all the publishers putting up individual Websites, journal literature is dissolving into incoherence. My sense is that most users do not structure their work strongly along publisher lines. Last time I looked, we did not have academic disciplines devoted to studying the works of individual publishers. Most people work in particular disciplines and most scholars, let alone most students, have not got a clue who publishes what.

One of our challenges, as we look at this evolving world of journals in electronic form, is how to recapture the progress we have made with the generations of online catalogs and their extensions. How do we retain coherence in our collections? I believe this is one of the most fundamental service and collection issues today. We are going to see abstracting and indexing databases form a spine that gives coherence to these distributed collections.

Saying this is easy. It sounds really good as broad theory, but some very complex issues arise in the practice. Linkage is one. We need linkage mechanisms between abstracting and indexing databases and these distributed repositories of journals that publishers are managing. This is not a simple problem. Check with your favorite publisher about whether direct addressability at the article level has even been considered. I have had some interesting conversations with people who build these Websites. I have said, "People want to make pointers directly into your journal articles so that authorized users might follow a citation from the bibliography of one article to the next article or make such a citation," and I've been met with blank looks. "They want to do that? We never thought of that. Gee, we'll have to redesign our whole system." Whoops! The primary question is do the publishers have the technical design to permit such access? The second issue is what the linkage mechanism is going to be. URLs? URNs? What kind of URNs? What kind of linkage code? A serial item contribution identifier (SICI)?

The next question is another good one. Where are these links going to come from? Some institutions have been building their own links. When I was at the University of California, we were tying up a lot of resources building links between A&I databases and publisher Websites. This is not going to scale. There is something profoundly crazy about having thousands of libraries trying to accomplish this individually. Links will have to be provided by the publishers, the A&I vendors, or from some third party. We are already seeing signs of all kinds of players trying to move into that area.

Another nasty issue is time synchronization. Abstracting and indexing databases trail the published literature by anything from a couple of weeks to a couple of years. The average working scientist is not going to be happy with a world of electronic journals in which access to information comes weeks after it would have come out in print because it is coming through the abstracting and indexing databases. The result will be a dual mode of literature access, in which most searching is done through the abstracting and indexing databases, but tables of contents for more recent publications will be found on the publishers' Websites. This will not be greeted with enthusiasm by most of our user base. They want a coherent approach to their research literature.

Solving this problem will require greater cooperation between primary and secondary database suppliers—between publishers and A&I vendors. It also has a serious operational implication for libraries. I think libraries have been amazingly casual about the time constraints on projects like database updates. Here is the scenario. You have an abstract and indexing database mounted locally. You get the update tape, load it overnight, maybe tomorrow, and nobody gets excited. Maybe you are loading weekly or monthly. The tapes come in weekly, but if they get held up in the mail for a day, nobody notices. We did not have that problem with primary publication in print. It came in and you got it out there. As soon as it was out there, it was accessible. If we need to update some kind of abstracting and indexing apparatus to make these new resources visible, users are going to be sensitive about how quickly it is done. We will have to get very serious about update schedules and time constraints in a way that we have not had to be. This wonderful world of weekly and even monthly tape updates in the mail is going to be replaced by daily or maybe even hourly FTPs that trigger processing programs when they come in across the Internet. It is going to create a new and different management world. There are many implications as we look at what the next generation of local systems look like. What do we want from our abstracting and indexing databases vendors? Now they are no more prepared to provide hourly updates to their database than libraries are to receive them, but I believe users will drive us toward this new world.

The final issue I want to raise about coherence in journal databases is coverage. We have several kinds of coverage problems. Abstracting and indexing databases do not cover everything in most journals. Some of them practice "selective" indexing. Some have selection criteria you cannot deduce. Some change editorial policies at least biweekly, and generally do not bother to tell you unless you pound on them because you noticed that something has changed in the latest database updates. We need to understand what we want and what we expect in the correspondence between the description of the literature and the literature itself in the electronic environment. The first step is getting informed about what is going on. We also need to think about what we really want. There is an additional factor. Contrary to what a growing proportion of higher education institutions (and particularly their undergraduate populations) in the United States are coming to believe, the published journal literature did not start in the early seventies. It only looks that way because that is the electronic coverage we have on it.

Incidentally, if somebody is looking for a fun study to do sometime, I would like to see an analysis of how citation in faculty publications or student papers at a given institution relates to how much of a backfile of A&I databases they can access in the relevant discipline. I suspect that if they only go back to 1985, or whatever the significant year is, one will see a sudden decline in the citations to literature published before that year.

The point is that we need to deal with retrospective conversion for the journal literature. The first step is getting some kind of bibliographic apparatus around it. Some efforts to digitize the retrospective journal literature—for example, JSTOR—are generating the abstracting and indexing apparatus for the material they cover as a by-product of their work. We will need to spend more time and money on the apparatus and less time digitizing, early in the process. JSTOR, wonderful resource though it is, has the same fragmentation problem. The access apparatus does not integrate reasonably with other A&I databases and the primary content is not easily linked to any access apparatus other than the one that JSTOR provides. It is an insular resource. Having a closed bibliographic apparatus that comes with particular runs of digitized resources merely contributes to the fragmentation of the research literature as it becomes digital.

Interaction

Another service boundary that we need to struggle with is interaction. We talk about the network as a publishing medium. In fact, it is two intertwined media, which are part of its richness and complexity. It is a medium for information dissemination and access and it is a medium for communication. Communication as scholarly discourse is moving into the network environment in more creative ways than just cranking up the scanner and transforming print pages into electronic pages. Interaction enters the picture very quickly. It is unclear how much we want interaction to come under the libraries' service umbrella. Many libraries struggle with the issue of whether their workstations should be public service points for general electronic mail transactions. Do we really want to host people chatting on the Internet all day long? What is going to happen when packet-type video technology becomes commonplace? Are we going to put little video cameras on top of all our public terminals and invite people to watch each other as they continue to chat on the Internet all day? This dilemma is not unrelated to that of people doing data analysis, for example, at public workstations. The answers are going to be different for different libraries.

One will see constant pressure to permit interaction because interaction is going to be more and more part of the new mode of scholarly communication and discourse. Content will be difficult to separate from interaction. Systems are now coming online that make this definition more and more confusing. Consider the experimental collaborative filtering or community filtering systems. Basically, either as a deliberate act or as a by-product of doing something else, you express likes and dislikes about some class of objects. This may be as simple as signing onto a system and typing in your ten favorite movies. Perhaps every time you read a Usenet news group post, you are invited to give it a rating from one to five, from truly memorable to truly useless, or anything in between. Many of these systems on the Internet take opinion polls for books or sound recordings. Some online stores are using software that catalogs this information. Firefly is probably the best-known company. People might visit amazon.com, for example, repeatedly making purchases and generating an information trail. These companies' databases compare the books you bought to the books others bought. If similar tastes show up, users might be solicited by the software to buy some book "that a number of other people with interests similar to yours are buying." These systems are still somewhat experimental. They are similar to some of the high-end, full-text information retrieval technology that respond to a few typed words. Sometimes magic happens, you get a really good, useful result, and you think it is wonderful. Then the next time you use it, it fails abysmally. You get a result so stupid and bizarre that you think the technology will never be ready for general production use.

This imperfect technology is something very powerful because it begins to emulate how human beings in communities find information. You ask people whom you respect, word passes around inside scholarly circles or other communities of discourse, and work gets a little buzz around it that causes people to start looking at it. This technology attempts to emulate such communication. How do these interactions fit in with library service offerings? Do we want to offer them inside library services? Keep in mind that whether or not libraries accept them, other organizations out there—in some sense, competitors to libraries—will offer this service. I don't have an answer.

User Privacy

Another related issue is how well we are really willing to get to know our user communities. In many ways, the less we know about our users, the happier we are. There are some good and legal reasons for this attitude and some tradition of defending user privacy: "Let's not collect and keep certain data, because if we don't have it the government (or other organizations) can't get it." The library community has kept this policy for all the best reasons, particularly to protect patron privacy. Yet in this new era, people are building personalized systems. The fact that these systems really know the users and know what they have been doing improves their quality of service. Current awareness, collaborative filtering, remembering what you've read, correlating it with other people, remembering preferences constitute a complex of systems and services that fundamentally rely on maintaining increasingly extensive and comprehensive dossiers on what users are doing, where they have been, where they are going, and what they are interested in. I think we need to grapple with that issue.

Clearly, you are going to build such systems with the informed consent of the user. Protecting anonymous access for people who want it is terribly important. As I look at the activity on the Web—for example, the changing relationship between publishers and readers—I am beginning to believe that within a decade, libraries may be the only place where you can look at anything anonymously. Perhaps bookstores and newsstands also will continue to fill this role to some extent. It depends on how rapidly and how much material migrates to electronic formats. There will be a class of information that you either will have to buy over the Internet with very little privacy from the rights' holders or read at the library. Anonymity may become a significant role of libraries much more so than today because so many other options are being squeezed out of existence. We need to address the service implications of truly knowing our users, not just their names and visiting days, but their research and their preferences, and getting that knowledge into our information systems.

Distance Education

As far as I can tell, many who are promoting distance education strategies either do not believe this or it has not occurred to them, but libraries are going to be an important part of delivering distance education effectively, particularly as it moves beyond very narrow vocational courses. Certainly, if you are teaching a class on photocopier repair, you can send out the manual and then give a three-hour video course without requiring library support. When the concept expands to projecting substantial parts of the higher education experience outside the walls of the university, you are going to need substantial participation from the library. We do not understand some aspects of this concept at all and we have made considerable progress on others. Libraries have been aggressive in getting a handle on the issue of electronic reserves, which can be used to support distance education programs. Different libraries have developed different policies, of course, and taken different strategies. This is an area that people seem to be comfortable addressing.

However, people are not so comfortable addressing one area. A lot of distance education is broadcast, and these broadcasts are recorded. This kind of information resource is going to be commonplace as digital video gets cheap over the next few years. Eventually, it's likely that every seminar and many classes at most major educational institutions will be videoed routinely. All this video will have to be cataloged and stored and someone will have to make decisions about what to keep and for how long. Is that a library function or can someone else take responsibility? Look at the EDUCOM National Learning Infrastructure Initiative (NLII). Information technologists and distance learning people are building an instructional management system (IMS), which they wisely did not call a digital library. Once people start looking at what it does, they are going to be very comfortable calling it a digital library. The relationship between libraries in institutions and this new kind of system is an absolutely open issue at this point and one that we really need to consider.

As video technology in education becomes ubiquitous, how will we organize, index, and provide access to it? Today, we are cataloging this information at a fairly gross level. There is a lot of technology in experimental development. One of the six NASA/ARPA/NSF digital library projects is the Intermedia project at Carnegie Mellon, which specifically focuses on what we will do with this flood of video. People are building systems that summarize videos, trying to provide key frames, trying to offer some framework other than the fast forward button for navigating through an hour of video that may contain something pertinent. Are we going to run these indexes in the libraries or will they be archived somewhere else? How well will automated systems, as opposed to intellectual indexing by human beings, perform? Instructional video material is not mass produced, as are books and journals. Copy cataloging strategies are not going to work because most of this will be unique material generated at individual organizations. This is another area that requires our attention as we try to draw our boundaries and set our priorities.

Special Collections

We know that a wonderful revolution is taking place in the realm of special collections. We are blowing open the doors through digitization and making a great deal of this fragile, hard-to-find, esoteric, unique material available in digital form to people through the Internet. No longer will researchers have to trek to individual institutions to mine the treasures of their special collections.

Undergraduates can enjoy the thrill of working directly with primary source materials. We are going to be digitizing away at these massive collections for the foreseeable future. Setting priorities and working through the process of digitizing all or even most of this material will take decades. We have taken some very important initial steps with projects like the EAD (encoded archival description) work and the electronic finding aids. These can provide a coherent context for ongoing digitizing projects.

Digitization of special collections will make an immense amount of previously remote material accessible and relevant. Perhaps a library has a special collection of a famous author. Perhaps a museum's special collection of an obscure artist contains important materials that relate closely to the first collection. These might be parts of a long correspondence between the two. Geography will no longer be an organizing principle for collections unless we want it to be. Somebody can build virtual special collections that bring together material from multiple sites. Who is going to do that? Is that a curatorial function? Is that a library function? Is that a function that is best left to the scholars? Who will maintain these virtual collections? Links die, links change, and electronic content needs to be maintained to be vital and useful.

A closely related issue is what to do about exhibits. Many large libraries organize modest exhibits and some support impressive exhibits. Museums, of course, offer exhibits all the time. Exhibits come and go. We can keep all of them, however, in the electronic environment, because we can re-purpose, re-arrange, re-present the same material multiple ways simultaneously. Such is the wonderful flexibility of the electronic environment. How much of this responsibility falls under the libraries' purview?

Preservation

That question leads me directly to the final issue—preservation of digital content. We feel philosophically and morally responsible for the preservation of everything, even if we are not exactly sure what it all is. Yet we are building systems, for example, the publisher-based Websites, that do not correspond to that philosophy. We are also missing something else. Our conversations about digital preservation are profoundly schizophrenic. Two separate conversations are occurring. One discusses information that is akin to the published literature but is more digital. We are worried about preserving it as much as we have always been concerned with preserving the printed literature. When we look at the scholarly journals going electronic, we continue to worry about how we are going to preserve them. While we have been worrying, a vibrant new communications medium has emerged on the Internet containing many new genres. As with virtually every new communication medium, almost no one has quite noticed it yet. We really do not understand the latest new communication medium any more than anyone had a good grasp on radio or television in the beginning. How much of the information disseminated from those media was archived in the early days? As we are discussing what is really important to preserve, lots of information is coming and going and going and coming and falling off the face of the earth.

In the 1996 presidential elections, both Clinton and Dole had Websites. Some scholar working fifteen years from now is going to be interested in charting how the world of the Internet and the communications that it enabled affected the political process during the 1990s. Such a scholar might have more than a passing interest in what was on those sites and how the site contents changed and evolved on a day-to-day or even hour-to-hour basis. Did anyone save them? I have not looked, but this scenario came to me when I was trying to think of good examples of event-driven material that is just coming and going on the Internet, and that we may one day regret not saving. We need a serious dialog about what our preservation priorities should be for these new genres. We need to look back to the last few new communication media to learn from our experiences.

Conclusion

I have made quite a survey here through various areas where difficult and controversial decisions are to be made. There are no absolute right answers here—at least, that is my view. Choices are going to be made by individual institutions based on resources, on expertise, and on the needs of the specific user communities that the institutions must support. They also will be made in response to visions of what libraries should become in the digital culture. There will be choices, not globally right or wrong decisions. Many of these choices are going to be about boundaries, rather than actions—about what organizations will not do, what they will define as outside their scope, rather than within their mission. I hope that this chapter has been helpful in beginning to define those choices, particularly for collections and services, and has offered some case studies that organizations can use to test their views of where their own boundaries should be drawn.

9

Licensing for Information Resources: Creative Contracts and the Library Mission

Kenneth D. Crews

Libraries' increased dependence on licensing and contracts for the acquisition of information resources represents a fundamental transformation of libraries from a collective resource into a node for the retrieval and delivery of information, often involving far-reaching locations. The dependence on licenses and contracts also reveals the increasing intrusion of law into the daily practices of librarians. Indeed, law always has been important to almost any enterprise, including libraries. It is law that creates the corporate structure and determines the authority of governing boards, that defines constitutional protections for communicating information, and that delineates terms on which libraries may hire and fire personnel.[1] The growth of licensing, however, is a reminder that the law now often affects the essence of our libraries. The license agreement for informational resources can define the terms on which the library may engage in its central mission of organizing, storing, and retrieving information for meeting the needs of library patrons.

Licenses and Contracts: A Legal Primer

The Fundamentals of Contracts

In order for librarians to maintain control of their central reason for existence, they are frequently responsible for understanding and working with the law of licenses and contracts in a meaningful and creative manner. Librarians need to understand the fundamentals and be watchful of evolving trends in contract provisions and developments in contract law. In general, a license is often a contract. "License" is used generally to describe a permission to use someone else's property. Perhaps most familiarity with this concept and term centers on licenses to use computer software—someone's "intellectual property." Yet the term "license" also is used for permission to camp in someone else's woods or to borrow someone else's car. Not all licenses are contracts. A license may be a gift with nothing sought in return. If it is not a contract, however, it is generally not enforceable if one party fails to deliver as promised.[2]

In the context of licenses for databases, software, and other resources, the license most often will be contractual. Each party is legally bound to fulfill promises, for example, to provide database access and to make payment. The law, when enforcing a contract, seeks evidence of a meeting of the minds among the parties. To find that meeting of minds in some objective manner and to identify binding contracts, the law generally requires three elements: offer, acceptance, and consideration.[3]

These three element may be manifest in many different ways. Negotiations, advertisements, or written proposals may be offers, with responses identified as acceptances. On the other hand, offer and acceptance do not have to be explicit. For example, the existence of a signed document implies that the parties reached agreement through some unidentified process of offer and acceptance. Thus, offer and acceptance may be inferred from circumstances leading to agreement.

The concept of consideration is more subtle. Consideration often is confused with payment or other return duty pursuant to the agreement. An obligation to make payment easily can constitute "sufficient consideration." In general, consideration is defined as the return benefit one receives for a promise, detriment, or obligation incurred as the recipient of a promise. For example, if a database provider promises access, it receives from the library a return benefit of promised future payments. Under the same agreement, the library also makes a promise of payment and in return receives the benefit of database access. In most simple quid-pro-quo transactions, one fairly easily can find consideration to make the contract. On the other hand, consideration may be lacking in transactions where, for example, the database provider offers samples or demos of the service, such as a trial test period, without obligation. Lacking any return promise, such transactions do not constitute a contract. When it is not a contract, it generally cannot be enforced under the law. Either party usually may terminate it at will without further obligation.

Authorized Agents

Contracts entered into by institutions or organizations such as libraries or publishers are actually negotiated, approved, and signed by individuals who are acting on behalf of those organizations. A properly made contract that will be binding against the entity must be entered into by an individual who has proper authority to act on behalf of that principal party.[4] Usually that authority may be implied by circumstances, such as the rank or title of the negotiating officer. Sometimes, however, the authority may seem to be valid on its face, but in fact it has not been established. One recent example raised in an electronic discussion group involved an Elsevier journal that a library purchased after negotiating with the sales representative for rights to reproduce and distribute the content through interlibrary loans. After the parties had completed their negotiation and reached agreement, Elsevier officials objected and asserted that the sales representative did not have authority to negotiate such variations in sales contracts. The agent's authority had limits. The lesson to any parties entering into an agreement is clear: ascertain through direct questioning who has the authority to make the contract on behalf of the library and all other parties.[5]

Unenforceable Contracts

Once entering into a contract that has the essential elements of offer, acceptance, and consideration, the contract may under extraordinary circumstances still not be enforceable. Many contract principles have evolved over the centuries to render some contracts "unenforceable" or "voidable." Most examples will have little realistic application to libraries. Yet the expansion of contracts as a means for acquiring information resources and the growing diversification of contracts raise more questions about enforceability. For example, a long-standing doctrine has barred enforceability of contracts with illegal subject matter. The simple, and albeit extreme, example is that of the drug deal. The offer and acceptance for purchasing illegal drugs may produce a contract by fundamental definition, but no court would ever find it enforceable because of the illegal subject. Somewhat more realistically, courts have barred enforcement of contracts by unlicensed parties where a professional license may be required to engage in that particular business. For example, courts may prohibit enforcement of contracts for construction or medical services where a contractor or physician lacks the required license.[6]

Conflicts between Contracts and Copyright

The issue of illegality of subject matter has been debated in the context of licenses for information resources that purport to contradict rights of use under other law. In particular, federal copyright law establishes that the copyright owner has a set of rights associated with the work, but those rights are tempered by fair use and other opportunities granted to the public. A license agreement typically may seek to alter that balance of rights between the copyright owner and the public users. An open question of legal interpretation is whether such a contract may be enforceable to deny rights of use established by copyright law.[7]

Those same circumstances give rise to possible unenforceability of the contract under other legal doctrines. Specifically, the conflict between federal copyright and a contract provision gives rise to a claim of preemption of state contract law by the system of owners' and users' right under federal copyright law. Conflicts between state and federal law arise in many circumstances. A long-standing principle of American constitutional law is that most such conflicts are resolved in favor of enforcing the federal law, which "preempts" the relevant state law.[8] Thus, in the given example, one may argue that the state law, which is asserted to enforce contracts, is preempted by federal copyright law to the extent that the state law might otherwise enforce a contract conflicting with or contradicting the federal copyright standard.[9]

No such principle is ever quite so simple. Under current law, one could hardly conclude with any assurance that licenses conflicting with federal copyright standards are therefore unenforceable. At most, the conflict produces an open question that can be brought into the negotiations in order, one would hope, to produce a contract that better anticipates and avoids possible problems. One also must be aware that no rule will ever apply in any easy, simplistic, and all-encompassing manner. For example, the more that a license has been carefully negotiated by the parties who have had an opportunity to discuss and object to terms, the greater the likelihood that it will be binding on the parties, even if the final terms conflict with copyright law.

The contract terms that are most often left in legal doubt are terms where the parties had no realistic opportunity to negotiate or to pursue alternatives. The courts have, in general, been reluctant to enforce contracts that would bind a party with heavily lopsided terms under circumstances where the party had no opportunity to negotiate or object or perhaps even to comprehend or investigate the terms before entering into the agreement. Such contracts are known as "contracts of adhesion" and they may well arise under circumstances such as shrink-wrap licensing for software where the ostensible agreement purports to constrain use of the program in a way that the user had no chance to negotiate or pursue. Again, court rulings that may clarify such principles are as yet in the future.[10] At this stage in the evolution of law and in the formation of contracts for library resources, librarians must become aware of the issues in order to prevent future problems and to recognize options in the process of negotiation.

The Substance of the Contract

Purchase or License

The terms of the contract are crucial to the library's success when entering into a valid and enforceable contract. A contract that constrains the usefulness of resources will prevent the library from fulfilling its mission of optimizing access to information. One central provision of a contract that can influence the shape of rights is whether the resources are acquired under a "purchase" or are a "licensed right of use." The distinction may seem only semantic, but it yields important substantive consequences. Under federal copyright law, a purchase of a work triggers the so-called first-sale doctrine, which allows the purchaser of a lawfully made copyrighted work to pass that work along to others.[11] Thus, the buyer of a book may resell it, the buyer of a videotape may rent it to others, the library acquiring sound recordings may allow users to check them out. If title to the copy, as distinguished from title to the copyright, is still retained by the vendor, the transactions may be a licensed right of use rather than a sale. Hence, the library as licensee does not automatically have the authority to pass that work along to others by means such as patron circulation, sale or trade to other libraries, or disposal through the usual process of weeding and discarding. If the transaction is a licensed right of use, those subsequent dispositions of the work are subject to the terms of the acquisition agreement or other approvals by the copyright owner.

This distinction between purchase and license has had important repercussions for computer software. For example, many software purchase agreements today do allow for the buyer to make a backup copy of the software to retain in the event of destruction or other loss of the original. Some software agreements, however, do not provide that right, but making a backup instead is allowed under Section 117 of the Copyright Act. However, the law grants that right to a *purchaser* of a software copy and not to a *licensee*. A recent court decision has affirmed that distinction.[12] Whether the library is a purchaser or a licensee of a work can make important and pragmatic differences in the library's successful deployment of that resource to preserve it and to meet information needs.

Contracts for User Rights

Contracts for information resources have vast and unlimited potential to define in wide-ranging variety the terms on which information resources may be deployed for advancing the library mission. Librarians must be aware of the simple fact that once a license or contract governs the acquisition of a resource, that contract is open to suggestions, revisions, and other possible negotiations, and it is open to most possible revisions to which the parties may agree. Librarians entering into these contracts have a duty to themselves and to their users to investigate alternatives and to preserve rights of use. At a minimum, librarians entering into licensing agreements must be aware of the basic rights of use that are allowed under existing copyright law and must seek agreements that preserve those rights, or even expand upon them. By way of example, the following summary identifies user rights that are crucial for many libraries, patrons, and parent institutions. An enforceable contract may expand or reduce those rights.

Preservation and backup copies
The Copyright Act, as described above, allows owners of copies of software to make backup copies for security.[13] Another provision of the law allows libraries under narrower circumstances to make preservation copies of some works in the event that the original in the collection may be lost, stolen, damaged, or deteriorating.[14]

First-sale doctrine
Also as mentioned above, this doctrine allows libraries to circulate works to patrons and otherwise dispose of them. Closely related to this doctrine is the increasing need to "transmit" works, particularly electronic or audiovisual works, that may be received by library users at off-site locations.[15] Transmission may not be explicitly within the concept of first-sale rights, but it is an indication of growing pressures for creative use of library resources, and the inadequacies of existing law, that need to be considered when negotiating effective licenses.

Displays and performance of works
One right of the copyright owner is to control the public display or performance of the works. Thus, in general, only the copyright owner may place a work at a location visible to the public or perform music or video at a theater or other place open to the public. Several important exceptions greatly facilitate public access to many works. For example, the owner of a copy of a book, artwork, or other copyrighted work may display that work to the public at the place where the work is located.[16] In other words, the bookstore or library may display its latest offerings in the lobby and a museum may hang a painting or place a sculpture in the open galleries. These rights are important for libraries that place art, manuscripts, or other works on public exhibition.

Classroom use and distance learning
A broad and sweeping exemption to the owner's rights of public display and performance allows instructors and pupils in the live, "face-to-face," classroom

to make what would otherwise be public displays or public performances of copyrighted works.[17] On the other hand, once the work is "transmitted" in the context of distance learning, the ability to make public displays and performances is conditioned on rigorous provisions related to circumstances as well as types of materials. Nevertheless, the law does allow, at least within limits, performance and display of works in the classroom and in distance learning.[18] A license agreement may be an effective tool for preserving those rights or for adopting alternative and more practical conditions for the use of works in distance learning.

Copies for interlibrary loans

Making and distributing copies of works for interlibrary loans implicate rights of the copyright owner. Yet another exemption in the law allows limited rights of interlibrary lending by qualified libraries.[19] Interlibrary lending, however, is sharply attacked by many publishers, and consequently licenses for information resources often restrict or prohibit the service. Continuation of interlibrary lending requires aggressive negotiation.

Fair-use rights

The broad and flexible right of fair use is often invoked to capture many uses of resources beyond the specific rights allowed under other exemptions.[20] Fair use is not without limitations, but it is still tremendously important for such common library pursuits as reserve operations, photocopies for instructional purposes, and access to media for teaching and learning projects.

Preservation of the public domain

Works enter the public domain for many reasons.[21] Some works, such as U.S. government works, are not eligible for copyright at all. Sound recordings were not brought under copyright until 1972.[22] Copyright protection for any work expires at some time. A great deal of public-domain material provides the foundation of expensive, commercial data products. A licensee for such products may be bound to restrictive conditions for using even the public-domain works accessed under the license. Libraries must resist licenses that constrain future benefit of materials in the public domain.

The essential point of this litany of public rights under copyright law is to identify a crucial starting point for the negotiation of effective and meaningful agreements for acquiring library resources. Contract negotiations should, at minimum, strive to preserve a least those rights of use already granted under the law. Negotiations also may build upon them to meet the growing and changing needs of the modern library. A problematic consequence of such a mix of user rights is that inevitably negotiations with vendors and other information providers will yield divergent results. For example, some suppliers may allow the use of their works for interlibrary lending, while other providers may insist on a waiver of any such rights. As a result, each work in the library collection acquired under a contract will be subject to its own distinctive rules. Effective librarianship increasingly demands not only the investment of time and scarce resources to negotiate contracts, but also devotion to the maintenance of contracts and to tracking the diffusion of individual rights and restrictions for the vast array of materials in a collection. This consequence exacerbates what Clifford Lynch has identified as a "sense of fragmentation" among our library services and resources.

Future Developments in the Law

The ascending importance of contracts, and the growing problems and complex questions they engender, inevitably have given rise to the proposal of new laws to further define this field. Therefore, librarians also have a duty not only to learn and apply current law in many fundamental ways, but also to stay abreast of developments in Congress and in state legislatures that may further affect the profession's ability to meet its basic objectives.

Database Protection

As of this writing, for example, a bill in Congress would redefine the scope of rights associated with a database of factual elements.[23] Facts and other points of information are not protected under U.S. copyright law. But an original compilation of those facts may have its own protection.[24] An electronic compilation that merely collects the information but does not necessarily select, arrange, or coordinate it in any creative fashion may lack any copyright protection under current law. That lack of protection is cause for consternation among database producers. The pending legislation, should it become law, would grant its own distinctive form of legal rights, but would allow narrow rights of use for research. Libraries would be compelled to reevaluate the terms on which they are willing to enter into agreements for databases.

Copyright Bills in Congress

Other pending legislation would revise statutes governing distance learning by making the law more flexible and by addressing more realistically the communication technologies for modern teaching.[25] Another provision of those same bills would make more explicit the right of a library to preserve deteriorating works in a digital format. These brief examples are simple demonstrations that the laws defining standards of use are flexible and subject to periodic revision. With each revision comes the need for libraries to reconsider basic terms for acceptable contracts.

State Law and the Uniform Commercial Code

As examined earlier in this chapter, contracts may be shaped not only by federal copyright law but by state law as well. In general, state law determines the conditions under which contracts may be made and enforced. An ambitious effort is currently under way to revise state laws regarding contracts for the acquisition of "information goods." Such law, if enacted by the state legislatures, would be a new phase of the growth of the Uniform Commercial Code (UCC). The UCC has been an important part of American law for more than a century. Its most important part or "Article" is Article 2, setting forth a long series of statutes related to the making and enforcement of contracts for the sale of goods.[26] UCC Article 2 has been tremendously successful for establishing continuity in the law of contracts throughout the country. It also has made the law better suited to the reality of business practices and more predictable for buyers and sellers of goods in transactions across state lines.

The new set of provisions, known as UCC Article 2B, is an effort to expand on that success by creating a body of law for transactions in information goods, ranging from the purchase of a book to the licensing of complex software and databases.[27] The proposed Article 2B is nearing final stages of formulation and may be offered to the state legislatures by the end of 1999. Nevertheless, the proposed Article 2B is highly controversial, not only because it represents significant change in business practice, but also because it leans heavily in favor of the enforceability of contracts, including shrink-wrap contracts and contracts that purport to redefine the balance of rights created by federal copyright law. Should Article 2B become law, it would greatly restructure the manner in which libraries will enter into transactions for the acquisition of all information resources.

Strategies for Effective Licensing

Whatever substantive provisions the current and future law relevant to contracts and information resources may provide, some strategies for effective licensing practices are becoming evident as libraries make the transition to the growing legalization of their daily practices and as they adjust to the increasing prevalence of contracts as a means for acquiring materials and defining library services. Five key strategies may help identify the ways a library can pursue its opportunities and fulfill its mission most meaningfully:

Identify the library's needs for the information resources

The ultimate objective of the license agreement from the library's perspective is to acquire the resources and to make them useful to library users. Thus, any meaningful negotiation of the contract must begin by identifying the desired outcome of the process—the library users' ultimate need for the materials. For an academic library, needs may embrace public performance and display of the works in the classroom and in distance learning, the transmission of the works to users accessing them elsewhere in the institution or from remote locations, and making limited copies of materials in support of teaching and research. Libraries of all types may need to emphasize interlibrary loans, public displays and performances, and preservation, among other issues.

Identify rights granted under existing law

This article has identified several of those rights provided to different users under specific circumstances pursuant to existing law. That growing and changing list of rights can become an effective starting point for negotiating licenses that preserve fundamental opportunities for the library and its users and that expand on them to meet important needs.

Develop baseline standards for contracts

Each library needs to establish in accordance with its own particular needs and objectives a set of baseline standards that it will expect to include in all of its contracts. That set of standards may be founded on rights granted under copyright law or special needs of the library. For example, the law provides little explicitly about the establishment of either print or electronic reserve systems or about the transmission of works beyond the library. If these activities are important to the library, their allowance can be included in the library's list of baseline standards or minimum expectations for an acceptable license.

Be prepared to reject offers and terminate negotiations

If the conditions for the use of resources are simply too restrictive or cumbersome, the library must be prepared to reject offers, terminate negotiations, or simply cancel programs. The exact breaking point between pursuing or terminating the transaction may vary depending upon the importance of the resources in question and the needs of the library. But at some point, the library must be prepared to recognize that the license does not offer satisfactory benefits and is simply not worth having.

Participate in national policy developments
Copyright bills cannot become law without approval of Congress, and UCC Article 2B is not law without approval from state legislatures. Librarians and their professional associations must make their views clear to elected officials in order to shape public information needs. Not only must libraries respond actively to existing law by negotiating creative and effective licenses, but librarians must also become more active in shaping and influencing future law.[28]

Conclusion

Contracts for the acquisition and utilization of information resources will be increasingly common and complex. Yet librarians have extensive opportunities to influence the shape of the law and the content of resulting agreements. Librarians must develop a meaningful strategy to make and implement contracts, and they may begin the process through a foundation of solid and critical information about existing rights and opportunities. Only through informed and creative negotiation and assertive participation in future developments will libraries best maintain high standards of service and serve the information needs of library patrons.

Notes

1. For an example of the growing literature of legal issues affecting librarianship, see Jonathan S. Tryon, *The Librarian's Legal Companion* (New York: G. K. Hall, 1994).
2. For a standard multi-volume study of contracts, see Arthur Linton Corbin, *Corbin on Contracts,* rev. ed. (St. Paul, Minn.: West, 1993–).
3. For example, Article 2 of the Uniform Commercial Code generally governs the making of contracts for the sale of goods, and it establishes a flexible conceptualization of offer and acceptance and the manifestation of agreement. In particular, Section 2-204 of the UCC provides: "A contract for sale of goods may be made in any manner sufficient to show agreement, including conduct by both parties which recognizes the existence of such a contract."
4. The law of agents and principals has been a fixture of the legal system for centuries. For a general treatise on the subject, see Harold Gill Reuschlein and William A. Gregory, *The Law of Agency and Partnership,* 2nd ed. (St. Paul, Minn.: West, 1990).
5. Naturally, the parties to the transaction are not likely to think in legalistic terms of agents and authority. Consequently, the explanation from Elsevier stated more directly: "It was inadvertently signed by a publishing staff member and it never passed through our Legal Department." Karen Hunter, Senior Vice President, Elsevier, electronic message to Liblicense-l list, July 25, 1997, archived at http://www.library.yale.edu/~license/index.shtml.

6. For example, see *Hydrotech Systems, Ltd. v. Oasis Waterpark,* 277 Cal.Rptr. 517 (Cal. 1991) (barring an unlicensed contractor from receiving payment even when defrauded by the other party).

7. In general, copyright law does permit contracts to modify, for the parties to the contract, application of the basic provisions of copyright law. The hard questions surround the extent of that permissible modification and the circumstances under which an enforceable contract may be made.

8. The issue of preemption of state law by federal law arises regularly. For example, the United State Supreme Court held that a Montana statute was preempted because of its conflict with a federal statute. *Doctor's Associates, Inc. v. Casarotto,* 517 U.S. 681 (1996).

9. The U.S. Copyright Act specifically preempts any other law that governs the set of rights granted to copyright owners for works that are eligible for copyright protection. Copyright Act of 1976, 17 U.S.C. Section 301 (1997).

10. One of the few cases to broach this issue is *ProCD, Inc. v. Zeidenberg,* 86 F.3d 1447 (7th Cir. 1996), in which the court upheld a standard-form contract against a buyer of a CD-ROM compilation of information similar to that in a white-pages telephone book.

11. Copyright Act of 1976, 17 U.S.C. Section 109(a) (1997).

12. Melville B. Nimmer and David Nimmer, *Nimmer on Copyright* (New York: Matthew Bender, 1997), Section 8.08[B][1].

13. Copyright Act of 1976, 17 U.S.C. Section 117 (1997).

14. Copyright Act of 1976, 17 U.S.C. Section 108(c) (1997). Section 108(b) allows preservation of unpublished materials under somewhat less restrictive conditions.

15. The Copyright Act gives this definition: "To 'transmit' a performance or display is to communicate it by any device or process whereby images or sounds are received beyond the place from which they are sent." (Copyright Act of 1976, 17 U.S.C. Section 101 (1997).)

16. Copyright Act of 1976, 17 U.S.C. Section 109(c) (1997).

17. Copyright Act of 1976, 17 U.S.C. Section 110(1) (1997).

18. Copyright Act of 1976, 17 U.S.C. Section 110(2) (1997). Digital Copyright Clarification and Technology Education Act of 1997.

19. Copyright Act of 1976, 17 U.S.C. Section 108(g)(2) (1997).

20. Copyright Act of 1976, 17 U.S.C. Section 107 (1997).

21. The leading reason for works to enter the public domain is by expiration of the copyright. Copyright lasts only for a limited, albeit long, term of protection. The term for most works created today is life of the author plus fifty years. (Copyright Act of 1976, 17 U.S.C. Section 302 (1997).) As of this writing, a bill advancing in Congress would extend the term to life of the author plus seventy years. (Copyright Term Extension Act, H.R. 2589, 105th Cong., 1st Sess. (1997).)

22. Sound recordings made in the United States are still not protected by federal copyright law if they were made before February 15, 1972. (Copyright Act of 1976, 17 U.S.C. Section 301(c) (1997).) Rights are extended, or "restored," for foreign sound recordings. (Copyright Act of 1976, 17 U.S.C. Section 104A(a) & (h)(6) (1997).)

23. Collections of Information Antipiracy Act, H.R. 2652, 105th Cong., 1st Sess. (1997).

24. Copyright Act of 1976, 17 U.S.C. Section 103(a) (1997).

25. Digital Era Copyright Enhancement Act, H.R. 3048, 105th Cong., 1st Sess. (1997); Digital Copyright Clarification and Technology Education Act of 1997, S. 1146, 105th Cong., 1st Sess. (1997).

26. See, for example, the provision mentioned at note 3 above.

27. For the text of the evolving drafts of Article 2B, see Uniform Commercial Code Article 2B Revision Home Page, http://www.law.uh.edu/ucc2b/.

28. Librarians, especially through their national associations, are active in many policy and legislative developments. One recent example is the Conference on Fair Use ("CONFU"), which included participation by several national library organizations. Nevertheless, the results of more than two years of negotiation produced results that most of those same organizations came to oppose. Librarians were represented at all stages, but clearly the need for involvement and influence is greater than what might have been possible in the past. For the text of the CONFU report, see http://www. uspto.gov/web/offices/dcom/olia/confu/.

10

Licensing: Pitfalls and Protection for the Collections

Karen A. Schmidt

Licenses have an impact on our users and our collections and affect the way in which we provide access. This chapter focuses on two topics: the way in which a library can handle licenses for the best review of the language and implementation of the license, and an inquiry into the changes and impact of licenses on users and collections.

Some preliminary observations are in order. First, the law does not keep up with social revolutions—it follows them. If one thinks about all the different kinds of social and intellectual revolutions we have gone through in our modern history, we will observe that it is not the law that is paving the way. The law simply does its best to keep up. The law is a wonderful interpreter of the impact of revolutions, but it cannot keep pace with these changes. Rather, it is a tool that often has to undergo its own revolutions for refinement. For librarians who review licenses, the lesson from this is to desist from having higher expectations than are warranted. The law often will stand in the way of the

The author is indebted to Kathleen Kluegel, University of Illinois at Urbana-Champaign Library, for the development of some of the ideas presented here. Kluegel's editorials in *RQ,* noted here, as well as conversations with the author, helped shape some of the points made in this chapter. See "Revolutionary Times," *RQ* 35, no. 4 (summer 1996): 1–3; "The Reference Collection as Kaleidoscope," *RQ* 36, no. 1 (fall 1996): 2–4; "Finding Our Way," *RQ* 36, no. 2 (winter 1996): 2–5; and "Redesigning Our Future," *RQ* 36, no. 3 (spring 1997): 2–6.

best interpretation of the use of an electronic resource, both in terms of our users and our collections.

Second, license agreements allow us to gain some degree of intellectual control over a multidimensional collection. The license agreement is part of the user manual for the electronic collection, telling the library and the user what it can and cannot do with a resource. In its particulars, a license allows the library to see how the collection can be used, both in its parts and its sum. For example, a license that is limiting may indirectly guide the library to supplement the electronic resource in some way. Therefore, for both collection development and for user service considerations, the library needs to understand the specifics of the license to gain control over these basic aspects of its work.

Finally, what the library bibliographer or selector may select is not necessarily what the library can procure. The selector may want services or access to information that the library simply cannot negotiate. Communication is critical throughout the acquisition and licensing process to assure satisfaction among all the sectors of the library.

A number of issues affecting collections and users need to be considered by the library when it handles licenses. These include legal issues, service issues, and collection issues, as described below.

Legal Issues

Three dicta emerge that serve as good guidelines for approaching the legal aspects of licensing. While self-evident, they bear repeating as the springboard to more complex arrangements and agreements:

Remember your lawyer is your friend

Every library has access to legal counsel and it is wise to make use of the expertise found there. As Davis and Crews so ably point out, licenses are complex legal documents that have binding powers over the licensee. Even in the event that a licensing agreement seems benevolent and accommodating, signing any legal document without counsel is unwise. Establishing good relationships with attorneys who serve your library is a fundamental step.

Learn the "vanilla" language and dispense with as much bureaucracy as possible

Licenses are full of "nuts and bolts" language that is recognizable, understandable, and negotiable once learned. The attorneys who counsel the library can provide this rudimentary tutoring and may allow the library liberty to change and sign off on licenses with contents that fall into this basic category. It is good practice to learn the legalese of licenses and what is required language for your institution.

Get to know staff in purchasing and library business affairs offices

Staff in purchasing and related offices often control payment and final oversight of licensing agreements and may have a different set of concerns about licenses than does the library. Thus, an adversarial relationship can develop if due consideration is not given to the work of these offices. These are important relationships that allow the library to establish productive connections with producers and vendors. When they work well, they are not noticed; when they do not work well, the library may find itself in a difficult position indeed, with delays in product availability and troublesome licensing issues.

Service Issues

User services are a critical component of licensing agreements and should be the focus of all negotiations. While licensing agreements commonly are considered by librarians in technical service or collection development areas, public service librarians often are most affected by the language and terms of the agreements. Public service librarians and staff are crucial to the negotiation of licensing agreements and they need to be actively involved in the process to represent the users' point of view.

Licenses can and do intrude on user services. They have a direct impact on authentication of the user, on numbers of simultaneous users, and on the platforms chosen for access to electronic products. As will be discussed in some detail later, these areas are significant operators in the ability of the collection and the library staff to meet user needs. If they are not fully understood and appreciated, and are not correctly negotiated into a licensing agreement, the electronic collection cannot fulfill its mission adequately.

Collection Issues

The collection development librarian already may be intimately involved in licensing review in your library. If not, he or she should be. As already suggested, the selection and procurement of electronic resources can be very different from print materials. Licenses redefine the collection and access to that collection in terms of content, archives, and the adequacy and effectiveness of the format of the information being made available. Many of the issues of concern to the user service or reference librarians are of significant concern to collections librarians as well. Consortial agreements in particular can set up a "one size fits all" situation that ignores the complexities and individualized needs of each library involved in the consortium. Collections librarians have a vested interest in seeing how electronic resources work within a macro-view of the collection of a library.

In short, a library is well-advised to establish a committee that includes all constituencies and stakeholders in the library and to provide a checklist of some basic issues that must be covered in selecting, negotiating, and providing access to an electronic resource. Such a checklist might include the following:

How well the electronic product compares to the print for coverage, indexing/ abstracting, and access

Who will review the licensing agreement

Who may sign the license

Who should be listed as the primary billing contact

Who should be listed as the primary technical contact—issues here include authentication, complete and correct IP address lists, password protection, and access to the resource on the Web page

Which company will provide the resource

In what format the resource should come (CD-ROM, Web, local load)

How publicity and training will be dealt with

When the start date will be

How information from the resource will be archived

Licenses: Changes and Impacts

The View of the Collection

Licenses and their potential restrictions may frustrate both the librarian and the user in a number of ways. The *MLA Bibliography* is a good example. When received as a paper copy, it allows only a single user but is a stable reference tool with predictable ways of accessing the information enclosed. A user will find exactly the same set of information, arranged in the same way, regardless of the library to which he or she goes. In the electronic environment, this same user will encounter a multiplicity of platforms, with various systems of entry and authentication to consider before the information is ever even encountered. The licensing agreement is one important component in easing the way through these potential difficulties. Certainly, if the license is not negotiated correctly, these areas will become increasingly impossible for the user to navigate.

Librarians handling bibliographic instruction are likely to discover problems connected with simultaneous users. How does a librarian teach a group of users to search a database when the number of simultaneous users is limited to, say, three or five? If hands-on experience is desired, the solution can be quite tricky.

Finally, if the license restricts ownership of the information on the electronic resource, if the library is merely leasing the information, how can research continuity and collection integrity be maintained? This is often an integral part of a licensing agreement, assuring the producer of continued ownership of the data and potentially assuring continued subscriptions to the database. Both situations are antithetical to the general notion of collection access and user service.

The View of the Reference Room

The reference room in the print environment is a physical expanse. Users frequently establish a relationship with a collection that is based on geography: the red books on the second shelf by the window, for example. Electronic resources upset that spatial orientation—the geography becomes less important.

The user of the electronic product needs to know where the computers are and what database they will access, but the singular configuration of one reference tool is no longer meaningful. Users will continue to relate to the computer in much the same way they related to the print item, but they will not be finding the same information. Various products will concatenate in a way not possible on the shelf. The licenses that represent these products will spell out how the terrain of the resources will be accessed and may reside and interconnect with other resources.

Relationships with Vendors

Vendors cannot, for the most part, serve *in loco parentis* for the library in the area of licenses. Producers want to work directly with the library to establish the ground rules for the product under discussion, and, even more importantly, libraries are almost never in the position where they can turn over legal responsibility to an outside party. This is a practicality not only in terms of the legal ramifications, but also because of the specific service issues that obtain in each library. This scenario might change in the future as licenses become more standardized, but for the present and foreseeable future, that is unlikely.

Therefore, libraries find themselves having to revamp their relationships with vendors. The book sellers and serial agents that have absorbed and supported so many library functions cannot yet compete in the area of licensing. Libraries still may use a serial agent to purchase these products, for example, but the library will have the extra step of handling the licensing agreement and may find working directly with the producer simpler. This situation becomes more entangled when electronic products are tied to the purchase of print items—the print may be handled through a vendor while the electronic product is handled through the producer, meaning more oversight on the part of the library.

Organizational Patterns of Communication

The need for both technical and public service staffs to embrace electronic resources and licensing issues has already been noted, but this bears repeating. Information has to flow throughout the different parts of the library for an electronic resource to be successfully selected, negotiated, and made accessible. Libraries need to turn traditional patterns of communication on their heads. These traditional patterns are based on the acquisition and service for print items, stable, physical, "ownable." Electronic resources, which often provide none of these attributes, challenge library communication and organizational patterns by switching from the acquisition of property to the acquisition of rights.

The user has to be included in the change in the pattern of communication. As the most important stakeholder in this initiative, the user has to be considered and given some voice in how these products are accessed and integrated into the traditional collection. The license, serving as it does as a structural foundation for use of the product, is an important instrument in this endeavor. For example, if a state university library has made a commitment that all state residents will have access to the library collections and services, the license of the product must allow this to occur. The unaffiliated user may never get an opportunity to speak to this, but the library must consider all users in its negotiation and not settle for lower standards of access. Licenses have to take into account adherence to these kinds of principles.

Summary

Navigational terminology is inevitable in speaking of licenses and electronic products, and the license can be perceived as the boat, and sometimes even the captain, of the product. The library decides whether or not it wants to give its users a canoe or a luxury yacht and whether users are going to go to Lake

Michigan or the Caribbean. The license is the vehicle for helping users over-come physical limitations to information, through adequate user authentication protocols, sufficient simultaneous users, and friendly platforms that work well with other platforms that might be in use in the library.

Libraries must recognize the power of the license in advocating for rights and accessibility to information, and to establish an internal routine that cuts across all organizational lines within the library, bringing in the legal and business sectors of the larger organization in which the library exists. We need to consider all the ways in which a license affects the collections, the services, and the users and to act on these considerations. As a significant and growing portion of the library collection, the electronic product and the licensing agreement that represents it are worthy of considerable thought and innovation on our part.

11

Legal Issues: The Negotiator's Perspective for Getting to the Heart of the License

Trisha L. Davis

Reviewing and revising a license agreement are an intimidating ordeal for even the most experienced librarian. With the assistance of an attorney, most of the legal jargon in any contract can be interpreted and modified satisfactorily. However, even the most skilled contract lawyer will rely on the librarian to understand and negotiate the product use rights and business terms in the agreement. To be efficient as well as effective in the negotiation process, the librarian needs to be aware of the pitfalls in reviewing a license. Rather than simply modifying the license agreement to avoid conflict, the librarian should take an assertive, perhaps even offensive, stance by focusing on the issues at the heart of the license. By modifying and amending the contract adequately, the librarian can assure that terms provide sufficient rights and protections for the library and its users. This chapter will provide the background needed to negotiate licenses for electronic information.

As with most negotiation, the best defense is a well-prepared offense. The librarian responsible for reviewing and negotiating the license needs to coordinate with other library staff to determine the library's overall policies for use of electronic products. Information such as the access methods, authorized user definitions, network security descriptions, and IP address structures should be formalized and prepared for use in negotiating license agreements. Once these basic decisions are made, the librarian only needs to identify any special use applications for the specific electronic product under consideration.

With the library's descriptive and policy information in hand, the librarian may review any license agreement simply by answering a series of questions about the licensed rights. If the contract does not provide the needed answers, the librarian may either strike or revise the existing language. If the question is not addressed, the librarian may insert the library's desired language at an appropriate section or amend the contract with the library's prepared policy or descriptive statement. This process of answering questions about the contract allows the reviewer to focus on the content of the license from the library's perspective rather than respond to the information provider's narrowly focused concerns.

The following questions provide an outline for defining the library's position in negotiations. If answered thoroughly, the reviewer will have the information needed to avoid common pitfalls hidden within complex license agreements. The preparation of the information needed to answer these questions also provides the documentation needed to assure protection for the library and its users.

Who Are the Parties
Involved in Negotiating
the License Agreement?

This seems like an obvious question, but in reality it often creates a major pitfall for libraries. Although the license agreement may name the library, or a library staff member as the contracting part, each library must identify and confirm its institutional rights to contract. Even a small library may not exist as a legal entity authorized to negotiate on its own behalf. In most cases, the party legally responsible to negotiate for the library is a city or county board, an educational institution, a corporation, or a nonprofit organization. Should the contract fall into dispute and either contracting party is incorrectly identified or established, additional legal problems may ensue. The best protection is a statement from the library's board or administration outlining the library's legal rights and relationships under the law.

What Exactly Is Being Licensed?

Many license agreements are written to handle a variety of products and services. Some contracts are written in generic fashion and fail to address specific details relevant to the lease or purchase. Having identified the nature of the product under consideration, the library should determine if the license adequately defines it. Many unsuspecting librarians have reviewed and modified a license received for a networked CD-ROM product only to discover at the time of negotiation that the provider required execution of a different contract for hard-drive loaded applications. A library with remote branches or regional sites may be required to sign the vendor's consortial license agreement, even though each site exists only as part of the legal whole. For protection, the librarian should assure that the correct contract is in hand and that all potential applications are covered.

What Is the Term of the License?

Due to the convenience of subscription-based payment cycles, a common pitfall is the false assumption of a specific coverage period or that the license agreement includes archival rights or perpetual access. Even the basic definition of subscription year should specify when the contract takes effect, the specific dates of product access or usage, and what volumes/issues/updates are included. For instance, a contract beginning on November 1, 1997, could provide access from that date through October 31, 1998, or it could provide the cumulative database as of November 1 and quarterly updates beginning in December and running through September 1998. Alternatively, the library might receive only four quarterly discs, beginning with the current disc, September 1997, and ending with the disc issued in July 1998, thus never receiving updated information after that time. For protection, the library could negotiate for the September 1997 update as a courtesy since the content already is outdated, but insist that the contract term include the four updates to be issued during 1998.

More seriously, many libraries have been trapped by false assumptions about licensed rights in perpetuity. Although some products allow the library to retain data acquired during the license term, unless the contract specifically defines archival or permanent use rights, none exist. Such rights must be spelled out explicitly in the contract and may require considerable negotiation to achieve. Unlike the acquisition of a subscription to a print product, the cost of electronic access for a single year may not provide access in future years nor allow the library to archive the data for use in the future. The information providers would like to require a current subscription in order to access the back files. As libraries move away from media-based products, such as CD-ROMs, and expend more resources on access rights alone, this becomes a major issue for negotiation.

How Is the Product Priced?

The relationship of pricing to licensing often is more complex than it appears. Many libraries have been trapped by false assumptions about the definition of terms upon which pricing is based. For instance, a provider may advertise widely that the product license includes network rights, but the contract defines the network in such a restricted manner that not all of the library's users have access. Even the concept of concurrent or simultaneous user requires investigation as some systems count users only after a search is begun, while others consider the opening of the welcome screen to be an access. Some agreements loudly announce that any number of B-level IP addresses may be provided, yet define *site* so narrowly that the library's B-level IP addresses cover too broad a territory, thus requiring multiple C-level addresses be authorized. If the pricing arrangements have been discussed, the library should not agree to them until the contractual definitions are examined. Better yet, the library should submit its own definitions of site, remote access, or concurrent user as a contract addendum to assure agreement is reached on the library's terms.

How Is an "Authorized User" Defined?

Each library has a unique set of patrons, which assures that most contract language will need careful examination and probable revision to assure all categories of users are included. For instance, "registered patrons" can include those with full or partial privileges, as well as special categories with unique privileges. If the library's registered patrons are not limited by place of residence and are allowed remote access, then the contract terms must not limit access by governmental boundaries or distance. Are currently enrolled students or faculty who are traveling abroad or participating in distance learning programs considered to be authorized with the same privileges as students on campus? Even though the university considers them to be full library patrons, the license agreement may prohibit their access by definition of site. How does the library present other categories of library patrons such as volunteers in the school library or business consultants using the public library, visiting researchers in the corporate library, or walk-in users at public terminals in the university library? Although the library may consider them legitimate users, the license may specifically exclude them. The only way to avoid such problems is to assure that the contractual definition of an authorized user is written in language that encompasses all necessary possibilities. If the contractual definition is too limited, the simplest approach is to append a clearly written definition of library patron categories. The majority of providers will accept such definition in place of the more limited, generic description provided in the contract. If the conflict is due to site or access mechanism, the authorized user definition can be agreed upon and the other issues can be addressed and negotiated separately.

How Is "Site" Defined?

As information providers have shifted from pricing based on concurrent use to site licenses, the concept of site has become one of the most complex and confusing issues to negotiate. Some vendors are concerned with geographical definitions, which limit access by the number of buildings in a complex or on a campus, by users within a named city or county, or even by users within a specified distance of the library. If the library's patrons are not readily defined by geographical boundaries, the best approach for the library is to select another method to define *site* or offer to pay an additional fee for access from all adjacent cities or an enlarged area of access. In academic license agreements, vendors often restrict usage to a single school or campus "under the same administration." Thus institutional branches, regional campuses, or remote classrooms may not qualify initially. However, a clear definition of governance relationships, noting in particular any shared functions such as registration, tenure, and granting of degrees, often clarifies the picture. Many vendors recognize that a smaller, more limited satellite office or branch could not afford its own product access and will allow services to authorized users in that location as part of the approved license. To be well-prepared for any contract negotiation, the library should draft site definitions from all geographic and institutional perspectives. The librarian reviewing the contract may then select the site definition that best meets the needs of the license.

What Use Rights Are Offered?

Many libraries make the simple assumption that the fair use rights provided under the copyright law apply to electronic products as well. What they fail to recognize is that once a license agreement is signed, contract law takes precedence. Thus, unless the expected use rights are clearly defined and agreed upon in the contract, they do not exist. To add confusion, contractual definitions often are so very specific they cannot be enforced or so ludicrously undefined that interpretation is unclear. Every license should begin by stating clearly that the licensee and its authorized users have the right to search the full database and display the results without limitation. If the desired product or database access is available in subsets, restricted by time or limited by content, these parameters should be clearly spelled out in contract addenda. Language that vaguely refers to key uses, such as "a limited amount of text," or is highly specific, such as "may be saved for 48 hours" should be examined and reworded to a more reasonable definition, such as a "reasonable number of copies" or "may be saved temporarily." More sensitive issues such as interlibrary loan rights or use of content in electronic course packs must be carefully defined. If the license does not address these uses, they simply are not allowed unless the library adds language stating them in terms that the provider will approve. The best approach is to request these use rights directly from the vendor in advance of negotiating the contract. In some cases, providing acceptable language from another vendor's contract helps with the discussions. The parties then have the opportunity to discuss the library's needs and define these uses in terms that are acceptable to both.

Does the License Allow the Needed Access?

A license agreement with the best terms for a product at the right price may not meet the library's needs if the access terms are not feasible or adequate for the library. The license for a CD-ROM-based product may allow stand-alone use and networked access from a CD-ROM player, but not permit copying of the data to a hard-drive on the network server. A Web-based product may be available through the library's intranet, but users who try to access the product directly at the provider's site may not have full services. Dial-in access for remote users may provide a seamless connection through the campus network, but not from a commercial Internet service. Each library must not only verify access rights in the license, but test them thoroughly during a trial period before the contract is signed. The negotiation for additional rights must include a definition of access adequate to meet the library's needs and the inclusion of those rights and definitions in the license.

What Are the Contractual Obligations?

Once the library's rights are defined, identifying any contractual obligations within the agreement is equally important. Standard obligations include the need to renegotiate the license if the access method changes, the requirement to alert the licensor to any end-user breaches that are brought to the library's attention, and a commitment to provide copyright statements on printouts. While these appear to be reasonable requests, the library should seriously consider the impact of such obligations and the ability to enforce them. For instance, the library could revise the license to agree to never delete or obscure any copyright statement provided by the product on any copies or printouts. This wording provides the same end result and security for the provider and the copyright holder, but shifts most of the responsibility from the licensee (the library) to the licensor (the information provider).

Standard business terms are appearing frequently in license agreements. The library should work closely with the business office and accounts payable to assure that any requirements are acceptable. For instance, an obligation to pay an invoice within 30 days of the invoice date may not be realistic at a large institution with multiple processing units. Modifying the contract, the library could agree to pay the invoice within 60 days of invoice date, or within 45 days of receipt. If an obligation to provide notice of cancellation six months before the end of the subscription period does not mesh with the library's budget cycle, the contract should be changed to a shorter notice period or the right to cancel if the budget is reduced.

Should Limited Warranty and Liability Statements Be Accepted?

As a consumer, the library has reason to expect assurance that the product being leased or purchased meets certain quality and performance standards. For the vast majority of print, audiovisual, and software-based library products, the vendor will automatically replace any damaged, incomplete, or otherwise unusable materials. For electronic products, however, no such standard practice exists. Some vendors will offer a limited warranty on the physical medium, such as the CD-ROM or diskette, and access to the data included. Even then, many licenses require notification within less than thirty days of receipt or they will not replace the product. Other vendors require a standard replacement fee for any discs that go bad. The librarian should review carefully any section of the license that describes warranties and replacement fees and not hesitate to remove objectionable limitations. If the product is Web-based, the refusal to warrant the product may extend to the availability of access. The provider reasonably can refuse to warrant access dependent upon the Internet, local telecommunications systems, and the library's network. On the other hand, the library can expect, or append, language that guarantees availability of service from the provider's network and/or Website.

Most license agreements will state specifically that no warranty is provided for content, currency, completeness, or accuracy of the product. While this may seem unacceptable, libraries have never had such warranties on print products. These terms are simply too extensive to warrant in any reasonable manner. What can be warranted, however, is the frequency at which the data are updated, and that content of the product will not be deleted without notice. Libraries should add language that assures the right to cancel for breach of contract if the data are not updated according to the agreed-upon schedule. Libraries also should insist upon notification of all changes to the database and that they have the right to cancel immediately if the database is reduced significantly, or even at all. Should the library choose to cancel for either reason, the licensor also should agree to rebate any prepaid fees on a prorated basis.

Liability clauses are not problematic as long as they are mutual. However, most indemnity statements are written to protect the licensor, not the licensee. Each party, the provider and the library, should agree to indemnify and hold the other harmless from any claim or loss caused by any negligent act or willful misconduct of the other. Thus the provider is protected from any claims caused as a result of the library's or authorized user's misuse of the product. The library is protected from any claims caused by the product, such as a copyright infringement, or by the provider's behavior, such as negligence, while on-site installing the product. No provider or library should accept responsibility or hold the other party harmless for any claim or loss for damages resulting from use of the product.

How Should Legal Terms Such as *Assignment, Termination Rights,* and *Applicable Law* Be Handled?

Most libraries, or their parent institution, will have written policies regarding the acceptance of standard contractual terms. However, the librarian reviewing the contract should understand these key terms and how they affect the library's license and use of the product. *Assignment* is the ability to assign a contract or transfer contractual rights to a third party, such as a parent company. Any assignment rights should be mutual and should never be done without notice to the other party. The library should never accept assignment rights without adequate notification and the right to terminate and receive a prorated refund of the purchase price.

Termination rights also should be mutual, that is, both parties should have the right to terminate the contract due to cause. The library should accept termination rights only if the rights are reciprocal, a reasonable notice of breach and the opportunity to correct any such problems is specified, and a prorated refund of the purchase price or any prepaid fees is guaranteed. In no case should the library take responsibility for end-user behavior or agree to licensor's termination rights based on end-use breach.

The final pitfall to avoid is controlling law and jurisdiction. *Applicable law* refers to the set of laws that will have binding legal force over the license agreement and any disputes over the contract. This clause always will be written to the benefit of the provider and may require the library to go to court in another state or to be judged by the laws of the provider's jurisdiction. The library always should either change the language to the state under which the library is governed or delete the paragraph in its entirety.

Is It Really Possible to Negotiate These Changes?

Yes, with careful preparation, solid negotiation skills, and a large dose of patience and tenacity, an acceptable license agreement may be prepared. In fact, many providers gratefully accept well-worded changes, attachments that clarify local definitions, and deletion of clauses that could prevent a sale. The confident negotiator is a welcome client who knows the product and educates the provider as to how to meet the library's needs. Most providers are eager to establish a solid relationship with such a negotiator because, in the end, the librarian's hard work and knowledgeable efforts benefit both parties.

PART IV

Understanding Change in Libraries: Implementation Considerations

12

Managing New Initiatives

Kären N. Nagy

Effective management of academic research libraries requires a new breed of leadership as we move into a new century. *Dynamic, visionary, risk-taking,* and *entrepreneurial* are adjectives that will describe the library leaders best equipped to manage change in an environment that often seems unstable and chaotic. The impacts and opportunities of new technology, economic pressures in higher education, and unpredictable costs and distribution models from the publishing industry drive much of the change *and* the chaos.

I will present three "case studies," very briefly described, from our recent experiences in the Stanford University Libraries as examples of managing change or effecting change within an academic research library environment. Each example includes nontraditional approaches to traditional library models or problems, many risks, and a number of significant opportunities. One example relates to major changes in our public service model and profile, another to substantial process and staffing redesign within our technical services units, and the third to a significant international publishing enterprise that grew out of strong local ideals. I will conclude with my own observations as both a veteran instigator and "nudger" of new initiatives and with twenty survival tips that are suggestions for managing change in academic research libraries.

Example 1: Changing the Undergraduate Library Support Model

In 1991, many of the front-end academic computing services were merged administratively with the public services areas of the Libraries at Stanford. Facing a second round of significant staff cuts mandated by university budget reductions, a major change to the undergraduate library support model was proposed and implemented in the fall of 1992. The J. Henry Meyer Memorial Library, built originally as an undergraduate library in the late 1960s, ceased at that time to house a separate undergraduate reference collection, reference service, and library instruction program. The libraries moved support services for undergraduates to Green Library and integrated them with the rest of the research library services delivered at that location. This change was discussed in open focus groups with both faculty and students and, while acknowledged to mark the end of an era of a special kind of support to undergraduate students, generally felt to be a desirable step given restricted dollars to spend on library staff and an understanding that Stanford undergraduates had long been using the rich and varied resources of Green Library and the research branch libraries on campus as well as the more narrowly developed Meyer undergraduate library collections and services.

With some minor physical alterations, this opened up valued central campus real estate for expansion of needed academic computing and instructional technology support services in the Meyer Library building. Over the past five years, an active and vital center for technology support to the campus community has evolved through the Research and Instructional Technology Support (RITS) facilities and services. The Meyer Library facility currently houses the media collections and viewing stations, large Macintosh and PC clusters, a language lab, an academic technology lab where faculty and students can develop multimedia instructional tools and projects, and a number of high-end technology classrooms. RITS serves as a hub for the academic community to facilitate the dissemination of technology on campus, often functioning in partnership with content specialists or other technology providers to integrate technology into the curriculum. For more information, see the RITS Website at http://rits.stanford.edu/.

This set of service changes, which seemed extremely difficult when we embarked on them, ultimately produced a win/win/win situation for the campus community. Duplicate reference services in buildings only a few yards apart were consolidated in favor of retaining a strong cadre of subject specialist librarians in support of the collection building and interpretation requirements of a research-driven academic community. Students, library staff, and teaching faculty reported a strengthened undergraduate library reference and instruction program through its relocation to Green Library's research reference environment.[1] A new set of computing and instruction technology support services grew up in a timely manner in central campus space. These services support dramatic emerging faculty and student needs with appropriate links to other library staff and programs.

Example 2: Technical Services Redesign Initiative

In July 1994, the Stanford University Library senior administration appointed a Technical Services Redesign Team to work with the Stillwater Consulting Group. This group was charged with applying the principles of reengineering to the acquisitions-to-access processing.[2] Their goal was to realize at least $750,000 in cost savings from the technical services budget, while maintaining or improving efficiency, speed, and quality of service. The redesign team represented a cross section of experience and expertise within the library system and at Stanford, including technical services librarians, selectors, a finance officer, and an information technology manager. The Stillwater Consulting Group facilitated the team's efforts and provided analytical support for process and cost examination.

The group developed a new model that questioned traditional thinking about technical services, examined fundamental approaches to processing incoming materials, created dramatically redesigned processes, and achieved a quality result less expensively. The redesign team's final report (January 1995) recommended a conceptual redesign that focuses on eliminating duplicate transactions, using technology and vendor services when possible to increase efficiencies, and performing tasks at the time or the location that makes the most sense. The redesign as implemented reflects a multi-tiered approach to processing that is responsive to the Stanford University Libraries' commitment to collect a wide variety of materials from different types of sources and that allows the libraries to cut costs by using vendors, technology, and streamlined processes to increase efficiencies.

Perhaps most innovative and certainly most controversial were the parts of the redesign plan that outsource tasks formerly done in-house to library materials vendors. The vendor-assisted tier includes components for both the acquisition and cataloging functions. Book vendors with interactive bibliographic databases, who can provide shelf-ready materials (including all number labels) and can transmit a stream of data necessary for the control and payment of those materials, are at the core of the schematic redesign for monographs. Current imprints and approval materials from our major United States vendor are the first applications of this outsourcing initiative. Bibliographic utilities that can manage the automatic recycling of searches for fuller copy and transmit the results of the successful hits are key to the cost savings for the cataloging functions.

Workflow redesign at the local level included consolidating processing steps and eliminating duplicate transactions by vesting responsibility for serials check-in and some record maintenance in service units. Development of technical support for the model has been based strongly on acknowledged national and international standards and protocols. A robust and flexible library management system was a key requirement for implementation of the technical services redesign plan, and those anticipated functionalities in SIRSI's Unicorn product were central to our selection of it as our next generation processing system in 1996.[3]

Example 3: HighWire Press Start-Up

In 1995, HighWire Press, a unit of the Stanford University Libraries, came into being as a visionary solution to a number of scientific scholarly publishing distribution and economic dilemmas with a lofty-sounding mission and goals statement. Three years later, its success is legend. HighWire Press seeks to partner with scholarly print publishers and to use innovative network tools for capture, publishing, retrieval, reading, and presentation of scholarly information. Its goals are to help ensure a direct linkage between the writers and readers of scholarly materials and to affect the economics of provision of scholarly information by providing an alternative to the semi-monopolistic lines of current science, technology, and medical research publishing. Effective online links among related scholarly resources in a given discipline are a core notion in the design of the HighWire resources. HighWire seeks to be responsive to scholars as authors by being an information technology partner to scholarly society publishers and to be responsive to scholars and students as readers, researchers, and customers by testing models, feedback mechanisms, and professionally done surveys. These particular strengths result from and reflect its strategic placement within the libraries at Stanford.

Beginning in its first year with a single journal, the *Journal of Biological Chemistry,* HighWire Press was launched through a small amount of start-up money from Stanford's president's innovation funds and a small handful of reassigned library staff members. HighWire Press is currently self-supporting with thirty-three journal titles online. Constantly adding staff and technical infrastructure to keep up with the incoming stream of business, HighWire now employs twenty-two full-time staff members, has sixty-five additional announced journal titles in the pipeline as well as others under discussion, relies on fourteen servers for its work, produces ten thousand print-equivalent pages per week, and receives 1.1 million page "requests" per week and 7.5 million user hits per week. Seen as a major force in the scientific publishing industry, HighWire's achievements and the strength of its presence to date are indicators that ideas creatively generated within libraries can have a resoundingly broad impact on scholarly communication issues in the networked information environment.[4]

These three "short stories" do not in any way do justice to the projects or initiatives they describe; if any one of these has piqued interest, the Websites noted above describe them more fully and adequately. Since these efforts were not achieved without varying struggles and challenges, they provide some lessons learned from managing change in a very complex and fast-moving environment. These lessons form the conclusion of this chapter. Following are twenty extracted "tips" based on my own experience that might be employed or expanded as others struggle with the particular challenges that increasingly put librarians in the role of change agent in their own institution.

Twenty Survival Tips for Managing Change in Academic Research Libraries

1. Work from principles or values to conceptual ideas to implementation strategies. This gives a solid grounding for decision making during every phase of change.

2. Feeling as if we are "making it up as we go along" is OK. The impact of increasing amounts of digital information, online environments to design and manage in the context of a local and international networked environment, operational models driven to change due to technological advances in the transaction systems used by staff and readers—all happening with rapid changes to the underlying technologies as well—have placed us in a planning and operational environment that often defies the kind of predictability we would wish for.

3. Repeat "there is no new money" as a mantra on the way to work each morning. Reallocation of resources is and will continue to be a way of life. If you are making good, well-planned, fiscally sound decisions, you may get money, especially for start-up or one-time initiatives. You must, however, build the capability for reallocation strategies into all thinking and planning.

4. Think through the kinds of expertise you need to get a certain task or initiative accomplished. This is a "quality" issue that is often ignored. Avoid least-common-denominator-solutions that may be the easiest or most comfortable to employ.

5. Allow no sacred cows. Give everyone in your organization permission to think in radical ways and to "zero-base" their planning initiatives. Promote an atmosphere in which the response of "we have to do it this way because we have always done it this way" is not rewarded.

6. Remember that stopping doing things is harder than you think. Start with the question "Do we have to do it this much or this often or this rigorously?" Then the question "Do we have to do this at all any more?" follows more logically.

7. Educate staff on the broader pictures in your organization. Helping people understand the context for their own work allows them to own the problems with more intelligence and promotes more creative solutions at all levels within the library.

8. Understand that people become worried about their jobs and their livelihood when redesign or reengineering begins being discussed in the workplace.

9. Be tolerant of different levels of readiness among staff members as they deal with change.

10. Don't use euphemisms such as downsizing or reallocation for staff cuts.

11. Remember: *training, training, training.* Help people understand that their basic skill sets still are valued. Give them the hardware and software tools and training to do their jobs well in new contexts.

12. Trust the faculty to behave like the faculty. Faculty often are primarily concerned about library collections as they relate to their own research and teaching agendas. Faculty support for the library is then a critical element that can be engaged in many ways toward promoting the interests of the library in any given campus context.

13. Help the campus user community understand that trade-offs are inherent in difficult decisions. Use terms they can understand. Elevate conversations that seek campus support for library decisions beyond library jargon.

14. Unrealistic and overly optimistic proposals are dangerous. Present choices honestly and be willing to deal with the consequences you propose without blaming others.

15. You can trust the university administration to behave like the university administration. Even with the best long-range planning goals, budgets and priorities within a university may change in a way that affects library support. Requests supported by data and ones that can predict multiyear needs can help to ensure even treatment during university budget cycles.

16. Leverage resources across lines that may have been drawn in the past—for example, with vendors for outsourcing, with donors or granting agencies for various kinds of support, with other service providers on campus, with other academic institutions or libraries.

17. Avoid foolish consistency. Question established models, whether in the ways budgets and staffing models are administered or in the kinds of services designed in response to discipline-specific needs.

18. Understand that we have mostly employed technology to "speed up the mess." In other words, first-generation technology solutions usually take paper processes and replicate them in an online environment. Be a change agent in your institution and use technology to get things done in different ways.

19. Consider using consultants to help plan or accomplish new agendas.

20. Allow the process of change to be flexible. If something is not working or not working well, know it can be changed again if need be.

Notes

1. Information about Stanford's undergraduate library instruction program and its strengths can be found at http://www-sul.stanford.edu/guides/beglib.html.
2. Michael Hammer, *Reengineering the Corporation: A Manifesto for Business Revolution* (London: Nicholas Brealey, 1993).
3. This text borrows strongly from the Executive Summary, "Stanford University Libraries Redesign Report: Redesigning the Acquisitions-to-Access Process" (January 1995). http://www-sul.stanford.edu/depts/diroff/ts/redesign/report/report.html.
4. HighWire Press's Website provides additional information about the press and its journals at http://highwire.stanford.edu.

13

Learning to Cha-Cha
with Change

Peggy Johnson

Dancing offers useful analogies for addressing change management and, more important, "dancing with change" sounds more appealing than the common images in much of the literature dealing with change. The typical approach in popular literature is to use intense, combative, and even aggressive images to explain change and individual response to change. These images range from white-water rafting to mastering change to getting on top of change. In this paper, I suggest that dancing with change is a much more positive and effective approach.

Marcus Aurelius said life is more like wrestling than dancing. Instead of wrestling through change, think about dancing with change. Listen to the rhythm and move in time. Dancing requires contact, but it is not a contact sport, and changing should not be seen as a constant battle. Change is part of life and one simply needs to learn how to do it more easily, better, and with grace.

My husband and I began our social dancing in the 1960s. This type of dancing required little contact and less coordination. Our approach to slow dancing was to put our arms around each other and sway. About ten years ago, we found ourselves at several events with dancing and quickly realized we were at a significant disadvantage on the dance floor. With much trepidation, we realized we had to change our technique. Bottom grabbing and swaying were not working. We signed up for community education classes and learned to cha-cha, waltz, fox trot, tango, and lindy. We have continued to take classes over the years. We are not masters, but we have learned various techniques, changed our style, and become comfortable with improvising. The confidence we have gained makes it much easier to change as the music changes.

This paper will explore change both theoretically and practically. The theoretical component will summarize how experts explain the change process and how change affects people. The practical component will address perceiving and reacting to change and how individuals might modify reactions and learn to dance with change. While this chapter does not consider planned organizational change, it concludes with suggestions for library managers as they help their staffs adjust to change.[1]

Change Is Stressful

Change is a stressor and stress is a physiological response. Stress is not always bad. Humans evolved to respond to threats as a way of self-preservation. If I encountered a wild animal, stress hormones immediately flooded my body, giving me the motivation and strength to defend myself or flee. My heart beat faster, my mental activity increased, my blood pressure rose, and my breathing became shallow. My immune system also became suppressed—possibly to make sure that if I received a wound, my immune system would not attack my own tissue while I was healing. These physiological responses to a perceived threat occur in any situation (physical, emotional, mental) in which an individual feels threatened.

The body has a three-stage reaction to stress: alarm, resistance, and exhaustion. In the alarm stage, the body recognizes the stressor and is prepared for fight or flight. This is done by the release of hormones such as adrenaline from the endocrine glands. These hormones are what cause an increase in heartbeat and perspiration, dilated pupils, and slowed digestion. The individual then chooses whether to use this burst of energy to fight or flee. In the acclimation or repair stage, body systems return to normal or pre-stress levels. The body repairs any damage caused from the stress. If, however, the stressor does not go away, the body cannot repair the damage and must remain alert. This plunges a person into the third stage—exhaustion. If this state continues long enough, the individual may develop an illness—short-term or chronic. College students often get sick as soon as they start a vacation and after their final exams are completed. As soon as the stressors are removed, the body collapses.

While the stressors or threats encountered today have changed, the body's fight-or-flight response remains the same. When faced with getting work done by an important deadline, an individual's body produces the same elevated levels of stress hormones that energize the dash from a saber-toothed tiger.

Because of today's accelerating pace of change and the uncertainty that accompanies it, many people feel stressed. When stress is ongoing, stress hormones are produced continuously, suppressing the immune system and leaving people less resistant to viruses and other illnesses. Stress is a consequence of good changes (getting a promotion, buying a new home) as well as negative events or conditions. The body's reaction does not distinguish between good stressors and bad stressors.

Thomas Holmes and Richard Rahe developed the Social Readjustment Rating (SRRQ) Questionnaire through their research on how people react to change.[2] The SRRQ measures the stress levels that external events typically cause. A cluster of social events that require change in ongoing life adjustment is significantly associated with the time of illness onset. These stressful events or conditions, the major areas of dynamic significance in the social structure of our lives, play a causative role. Some are negative or stressful in the conventional sense, and many are socially desirable. What they have in common is that each usually evokes or is associated with some adaptive or coping behavior on the part of the involved individual. Each event either is indicative of or requires a significant change in the ongoing life pattern of the individual. The scale value of each event reflects the degree of disruption it causes in the average person's life. It represents the average amount, severity, or duration of personal adjustment required to restore equilibrium after experiencing the event. The value is assigned according to degree of change from the existing steady state and not on psychological meaning, emotion, or desirability. For example, while the death of a spouse is a high stressor, so also is getting a significant promotion at work.

Figure 1 is proposed as one possible SRRQ for librarians. The list of stressor events was created through discussions with colleagues and personal experience. It has not been tested and has no scientific pretensions, yet one can posit that the closer one's total score gets to 500, the greater the physical risk. While this hypothetical SRRQ is intended for individual consideration, it also might be viewed as a library's rating. The implications for the organizational health of the library experiencing these changes are equally noteworthy.

Listed in figure 1 are many library events that simulate stress reactions in individual library staff members. The scale value of each event reflects a suggested degree of disruption it causes in the average person's life; that is, it represents the average amount, severity, or duration of personal adjustment to restore equilibrium.

Libraries face an unprecedented amount of change today. Much of this change is technology related. The stress produced has its own name—technostress. Most of the chapters in this book focus on significant technologically induced changes affecting society, libraries, and those who work in libraries. Our future success as organizations and as individuals—even our personal health

Implementation of automated library system	100
Implementation of a replacement automated system or major enhancement/upgrade	80
New boss	50
Promotion, reclassification to higher class, tenure awarded	50
Major change in responsibilities at work	39
Outstanding personal achievement	35
New co-worker(s)	30
Begin or end of formal schooling	25
Major project assigned or completed	25
Trouble with boss	23
Change in work hours or physical conditions in work environment	20
Minor change in responsibilities at work	19
Assigned responsibility of chairing a new committee	16
Vacation	13
TOTAL	525

(See Thomas H. Holmes and R. H. Rahe, "The Social Readjustment Rating Scale," *Journal of Psychosomatic Research* 11 (August 1967): 213–18, for original research using this instrument.)

Figure 1. Librarian's Social Readjustment Rating Questionnaire

and well-being—will depend upon how well we can manage and anticipate change at all levels of the organization.

Change Theory

Change has two important characteristics that are not mutually exclusive. First, change is ongoing, constant, and occurring at an unprecedented rate. It is inevitable. Some change is planned, but not all change is planned, directed, and controlled. Peter Vaill called the turbulence in our environment "permanent white water."[3] Second, change is not an event, but a process. In other words, every change we experience has stages or phases through which it can be defined. Most change literature defines change, both personal and organizational, in three stages. Kurt Lewin, one of the most respected change theorists, uses the three terms of unfreezing, moving, and refreezing to describe this three-stage process.[4] The three stages are assigned various terms by others; figure 2 compares vocabularies of other change theorists.[5]

Author	First Stage	Middle Stage(s)	Final Stage
Lewin	unfreezing	transition or moving	refreezing
Bridges	endings	neutral zone	beginnings
Tuckman	storming	norming	reforming
Barczak et al.	pattern breaking	experimenting and visioning	bonding and attunement
Kuhn	growth of anomalies	crisis, revolution	normal science within new paradigm
Marx	growing dissatisfaction	conflicts, crisis, revolution	new order

Figure 2. Change Theory

Unfreezing or ending is the state in which people identify what is ending, what they might be losing by the change, and what can be preserved to take along to the "new world" in the transition. The forces for change increase or the forces resisting change decrease, opening the way for change. Unfreezing is followed by an in-between stage or the neutral zone. This is a period of moving or transition and can be characterized by confusion and ambiguity. For others, it may be a time of energy and creativity. Transition cannot be abridged before the next stage, beginnings, is reached. If it is shortened or rushed, a true transition has not taken place. This is one reason that new widows or widowers are encouraged not to make dramatic changes too quickly and to allow sufficient time for grieving. Transition involves analyzing, designing, developing, and installing a new system or understanding to move to a new level of equilibrium. In the refreezing or ending stage, people are prepared and ready to address the new. They can be constructive about the change, if they have had enough of a transition period preceding it. They adjust to the new level through balancing a new set of equal and opposing forces. At this point, the new system is institutionalized and equilibrium is reached.

Unfreezing current behavior, understanding, or perceptions is complicated and often difficult. It requires addressing a web of interlocking variables that may include a formal reward system, social reinforcement from a peer group, defense mechanisms used to protect against psychological threat, cues and props in the surrounding environment, and individual conceptions of proper role behavior. Any stimulus for change that does not alter the affecting variables will either be resisted or, at the most, cause only temporary or cosmetic change. Once the unfreezing process has occurred, the individual can see new patterns of behavior or understanding as clear and attractive along with rationale for moving in this direction. Finally, the new behavior, understanding, or perception must undergo refreezing. If they are to endure, they must be supported by social cues and formal and informal reward systems.

Library cataloging units have gone through significant changes over the last twenty-five years. The following story demonstrates the three stages of change. After decades of creating catalog cards, a cataloging unit began using OCLC and MARC format for cataloging. Initially, the catalogers could not conceptualize the cataloging process without the 3-by-5 cards on which to lay out the familiar format with its prescribed indentations, punctuation, and so on. Over time, however, reasons to think of cataloging in terms of MARC tags appeared. This was how the catalogers' colleagues discussed cataloging and this was how they themselves communicated with the automated system. Their behaviors began to unfreeze as they realized their present cataloging practices were not as effective as the new approach. They moved to the new methods gradually, first annotating cards with the fields and tags, then creating catalog records in MARC format on worksheets, finally creating catalog records directly online. Eventually, they had fully integrated the new way of cataloging into their routine activities. This new approach no longer seemed radical or suspect, and the catalogers' cataloging practices were refrozen in a new behavior. Change theory emphasizes that the status quo or stability must be disturbed before change begins. In other words, change is impossible without change.

Change in organizations is intensely personal and at the same time, systemic. People going through each of these stages will experience change in different ways, depending on their view of the reasons for and the goal of the change, their understanding of it, their readiness for it, and whether they initiated it. Each individual in an organization is experiencing different changes and is at different stages in adapting to each of those changes. These variations add to the complexities of organizational behavior. Change becomes particularly problematic and stressful if one is unable to move into the refreezing or ending stage, but must start over again accommodating another change. This increases the turmoil, tension, and stress.

Resisting Change

Rosabeth Moss Kanter has identified ten common reasons for reluctance to change.[6] She suggests that one or more of the following factors are at the heart of all resistance.

1. Loss of control and feeling of powerlessness
2. Excess uncertainty
3. Surprise

4. Difference effect—one becomes conscious of and questions the familiar
5. Loss of face
6. Concerns about future competence
7. Ripple effects—one fears other disruptions will follow
8. More work requiring more energy, more time, and greater mental effort
9. Past resentments
10. Impact, fear, or threat is real

Resistance to change is often a nearly automatic attempt at self-protection. Most of Kanter's factors describe perceived or actual risk. Change is stressful, and refusing to accommodate change may seem easier, safer, and more comfortable. However, all change, even devastating change, offers an opportunity to learn and grow. How we do that is separate from the change itself and is totally dependent upon how people move through the transition stage. Transition is a period of reorientation during which people seek new meanings and ways to function in a changing situation. They seek new ways to define themselves in relation to their changing environment.

In transition or the neutral zone, people ask questions to gain understanding about why the change is necessary. They want to know what was wrong with the old way and why the new way is better. An individual in transition needs confidence that letting go of the old is wise. The neutral zone is marked by chaos and confusion. Change is difficult because it requires letting go, which leads to a high level of emotional stress. The more one identifies with that which is changing and the less ownership one has of the change, the more stressful letting go is. Change is the most stressful if it is done to and not initiated by the person experiencing it. We define ourselves through our work, which gives a sense of identity and worth. A major change in a job or the way it must be performed can conflict with self-image and sense of value both for the organization and for ourselves.

People act out their resistance to change in common ways. Many changes in rapid succession can result in people becoming disoriented. People need sufficient transition time to become reoriented before dealing with a new set of changes. A steady stream of unrelated or rapid changes can be confusing. Without time to absorb and adjust, individuals do not know what to do. They ask many questions, both because they need the answers to proceed and because they want extra time.

Some people consciously and directly resist change. Their resistance is active and deliberate. They are the ones who tell everyone the new approach is sure to fail or that it was tried before and failed the last time. Others try to ignore the change. They stay in a state of denial as long as possible. If I deny it, then I don't have to deal with it. If I delay the change, I can avoid it for a while longer. Both active and passive resistance can feel safer than the risk of changing.

Change and the resulting stress can produce a high level of energy. When the response is resistance, it is accompanied by emotions of worry, anger, frustration, and depression. Negative emotional responses complicate the transition period because individuals cannot direct energy to answering questions, processing answers, and moving on. Stress permeates the environment, people become more difficult to work with, and interpersonal relationships suffer.

Some behaviors in response to change are positive. The increased mental activity and energy that result from stressing experiences can generate creativity and enthusiasm. Some people might even be considered change "junkies" because they find change stimulating in a very positive and productive way. Others who encounter change more cautiously still may move through the three stages with supporting and encouraging behaviors. They accept that moving through transitions leads to new insights. Change can be difficult and stressful, but it is also the only way things improve. To put it another way—it won't get better unless it changes.

Managing Change

While change is inevitable, individuals always can choose how they respond. They can fight with change or dance with it. One can choose to meet a change with constructive energy and to take control. Sometimes one can lead the dance; other times one should follow. Accommodating change does not mean a loss of power. When an individual takes responsibility for personal reactions, he or she ceases to be a victim. Even in situations in which an individual has no say in the change being implemented, he or she has power over personal responses. When dealing with the stresses of life, perception is everything. If an individual perceives a situation as threatening—a deadline, a traffic jam, the automated system going down, giving a speech—the body will respond to it as threatening. While one does not always have control over stressful situations, one does have some control over reactions to them. Being conscious of and managing one's reactions can provide a sense of control.

Several writers have suggested techniques for coping with change.[7] Change involves letting go of the old, and this leads to a sense of loss and grief. Accept this feeling of loss as part of change. Feel free to express nostalgia for the past and honor it. At the same time, envision the future in a positive manner. Celebrate both that which is ending and that which is beginning. Avoid endless commiseration, but realize that constructive talk about the change with work peers or with a spouse or significant other can put it in perspective. Cultivate a healthy lifestyle through good diet, sufficient rest, and regular physical exercise to build resistance to the stress that change causes. When the new seems overwhelming, shift to a different work task or, when possible, an engrossing nonwork activity. Withdraw physically from the situation—take a walk! Engaging in regular meditation, prayer, or another form of mental relaxation is helpful. Analyze the situation, and change strategies to accommodate the change. Recognize what can be controlled and what cannot—and do not waste energy on the latter. Learn to accept what is beyond your control. Try to focus on one thing at a time. Try to see change as an opportunity for learning and growth. Understand the three stages of change and your progress through each. Allow time to move through each stage. Find out as much as possible about the change. Be clear on what you want and what is important to you. Know your strengths and weaknesses. Use your strengths to manage what you can manage and control.

Organizational Change

This paper has focused on how the individual experiences change and how the individual can move through changes with skill and grace. Those charged with implementing library changes—from new automated systems to new organizational structures to reference services via the World Wide Web—can apply the ideas presented here. Reviewing the reasons people resist change suggests appropriate techniques. Begin by making clear the reasons for the change and what it will accomplish. People react poorly to surprises. Continue to share information about progress, but don't overwhelm people. Continuous, but not continual, communication is the key to addressing the uncertainty with which people react to change.

Convey a sense of urgency. This may be either a crisis that has to be overcome or an opportunity that should not be missed. Create a vision that will guide the change effort and strategies for achieving that vision. In other words, the purpose must be clear in order for staff members to have a shared, understood goal. Provide incentives. Plan for and create opportunities for short-term wins. Celebrate accomplishments, both big and small. Congratulate people for their successes. At the same time, make clear the consequences to the individual and the library if the change is not implemented successfully.

Provide staff members with the chance to collaborate or participate in planning or implementing the change. This can alleviate feelings of powerlessness and loss of control. This does not mean that decisions have to be based on consensus. The change project must have a champion or leader and a team or group with enough power to direct the change effort. Lines of responsibility for the change being implemented should be clear, but avoid rigid, restricted boundaries. Everyone remains responsible for their own duties, but each is encouraged to create a common understanding of the entire task. Treat everyone with respect, tolerance, and trust, and foster this attitude among all staff members. Realize that people react to change differently and adapt at different rates. Provide time to mourn what is passing. Be patient.

People must feel competent to deal with the change and the problems they face in implementing it. Training is critical if the library is to address individuals' fear of failure and losing face. Allow sufficient implementation time and remember that every project takes twice as long as projected. Move through the implementation in phases. Incremental implementation is much more tolerable than instantaneous, comprehensive change. Provide people with the opportunity to do what they know how to do as they move into new tasks and new procedures and a new environment.

Conclusion

Change is inevitable. Automation-induced change is pervasive and constant in libraries. We must learn how to accommodate it productively and gracefully. Understanding the three stages of change—unfreezing, transition, and refreezing—provides an important perspective on managing change. We can make personal choices about how we react to change, what we perceive as stressful, and how we handle stress. Dealing with rapid and constant change does not have to be a wrestling match or white-water rafting. We can learn to dance with change by monitoring and adjusting how we adapt.

Notes

1. The interested reader is directed to an extensive and lively body of literature on organizational change; see, for example, the following recent works: John P. Kotter, "Leading Change: Why Transformation Efforts Fail," *Harvard Business Review* 73 (1995): 603–31; Robert J. Marshak, "Managing the Metaphors of Change," *Organizational Dynamics* 22 (1993): 44–56; Vernon D. Miller, John R. Johnson, and Jennifer Grau, "Antecedents to Willingness to Participate in a Planned Organizational Change," *Journal of Applied Communication Research* 22 (1994): 59–80; and Robert H. Schaffer and Harvey A. Thomson, "Successful Change Programs Begin with Results," *Harvard Business Review* 70 (1992): 80–89.
2. Thomas H. Holmes and R. H. Rahe, "The Social Readjustment Rating Scale," *Journal of Psychosomatic Research* 11 (August 1967): 213–18.
3. Peter B. Vaill, *Learning as a Way of Being: Strategies for Survival in a World of Permanent White Water* (San Francisco: Jossey-Bass, 1996).

4. Kurt Lewin, "Frontiers in Group Dynamics: Concepts, Method, and Reality in Social Sciences: Social Equilibria and Social Change," *Human Relations* 1 (June 1947): 5–41.

5. Figure 2 drawn from the works of Kurt Lewin; William Bridges, "Managing Organizational Transitions, *Organizational Dynamics* 15, no. 1 (summer 1986): 24–33; Bruce W. Tuckman, "Developmental Sequence in Small Groups," *Psychological Bulletin* 63, no. 6 (1965): 384–99; Gloria Barczak, Charles Smith, and David Wilemon, "Managing Large-Scale Organizational Change," *Organizational Dynamics* 16 (autumn 1987): 23–35; Thomas Kuhn, *The Structure of Scientific Revolution,* 2nd ed. (Chicago: University of Chicago Press, 1970); Karl Marx, *Capital, the Communist Manifesto, and Other Writings,* ed. Max Eastman (New York: Modern Library, 1959).

6. Rosabeth Moss Kanter, "Managing the Human Side of Change," *Management Review* 74 (April 1985): 52–56.

7. Techniques suggested here are adapted from those suggested by Rosabeth Moss Kanter, op. cit; Judy Clark, "Understanding Transition: The People Side of Managing Change," *Serials Librarian* 25, no. 3/4 (1995): 193–202; Daryl R. Conner, *Managing at the Speed of Change* (New York: Villard Books, 1993); and personal experience.

Bibliography

"The American Academic Profession." *Daedalus* 126, no. 4 (fall 1997).

Atkinson, Ross. "The Academic Library Collection in an On-Line Environment." In *Information Technology and the Remaking of the University Library,* ed. Beverly P. Lynch, 43–62. New Directions for Higher Education, no. 90. San Francisco: Jossey-Bass, 1995.

———. "Access, Ownership, and the Future of Collection Development." In *Collection Management and Development: Issues in an Electronic Era,* ed. Peggy Johnson and Bonnie MacEwan, 92–119. ALCTS Papers on Library Technical Services and Collections, no. 5. Chicago: American Library Association, 1994.

———. "Acquisitions Librarian as Change Agent in the Transition to the Electronic Library." *Library Resources & Technical Services* 36 (January 1992): 11–15.

———. "Networks, Hypertext, and Academic Information Services: Some Longer-Range Implications." *College & Research Libraries* 54 (May 1993): 208.

Barczak, Gloria, Charles Smith, and David Wilemon. "Managing Large-Scale Organizational Change." *Organizational Dynamics* 16 (autumn 1987): 23–35.

"Books, Bricks, and Bytes." *Daedalus* 125, no. 4 (fall 1996).

Bridges, William. "Managing Organizational Transitions." *Organizational Dynamics* 15, no. 1 (summer 1986): 24–33.

Cannon, David. "Generation X: The Way They Do the Things They Do." *Journal of Career Planning and Employment* 51 (1991): 34–38.

Carpenter, Kenneth E. "A Library Historian Looks at Librarianship." *Daedalus* 125 (fall 1996): 77–102.

Clack, Mary Elizabeth. "Managing Organization Change: The Harvard College Library Experience." *Serials Librarian* 25, no. 3/4 (1995): 149–61.

Clark, Judy. "Understanding Transition: The People Side of Managing Change." *Serials Librarian* 25, no. 3/4 (1995): 193–202.

Cline, Nancy M. "Staffing: The Art of Managing Change." In *Collection Management and Development: Issues in an Electronic Era,* ed. Peggy Johnson and Bonnie MacEwan, 13–28. ALCTS Papers on Library Technical Services and Collections, no. 5. Chicago: American Library Association, 1994.

"CONFU: Conference on Fair Use." http://www.uspto.gov/web/offices/dcom/olia/confu/

Conner, Daryl R. *Managing at the Speed of Change.* New York: Villard, 1993.

Corbin, Arthur Linton. *Corbin on Contracts.* Rev. ed. St. Paul, Minn.: West, 1993– .

Dannelly, Gay. "Resource Sharing in the Electronic Era: Potentials and Paradoxes." *Library Trends* 43 (spring 1985): 663–78.

Davis, Trisha. "License Agreements in Lieu of Copyright: Are We Signing Away Our Rights?" *Library Acquisitions: Practice and Theory* 21 (spring 1997): 19–28.

Deekle, Peter V., and Ann DeKlerk. "Perceptions of Library Leadership in a Time of Change." *Journal of Library Administration* 17, no. 1 (1992): 55–75.

De Meuse, Kenneth P., and Kevin K. McDaris. "An Exercise in Managing Change." *Training and Development* 48, no. 2 (Feb. 1994): 55–57.

Dowlin, Kenneth E. *The Electronic Library: The Promise and the Process.* New York: Neal-Schuman, 1984.

Eco, Umberto. "Afterword." In *The Future of the Book,* ed. Goeffrey Nunberg. Berkeley: University of California Press, 1996.

Ferguson, Anthony W. "Collection Development Politics: The Art of the Possible." In *Collection Management and Development: Issues in an Electronic Era,* ed. Peggy Johnson and Bonnie MacEwan, 29–41. ALCTS

Papers on Library Technical Services and Collections, no. 5. Chicago: American Library Association, 1994.

Gardner, John W. *Building Community.* Palo Alto, Calif.: Leadership Studies Program of the Independent Sector, 1991.

Hall, Blaine H. *Collection Assessment Manual for College and University Libraries.* Phoenix: Oryx, 1985.

Harloe, Bart, and John M. Budd. "Collection Development and Scholarly Communication in the Era of Electronic Access." *Journal of Academic Librarianship* 20 (May 1994): 83–87.

Henderson, Tona, and Bonnie MacEwan. "Electronic Collection and Wired Faculty." *Library Trends* 45, no. 3 (1997): 488–98.

Hernon, Peter, and Charles R. McClure. *Improving the Quality of Reference Service for Government Publications.* Chicago: American Library Association, 1983.

Hesse, Carla. "Books in Time." In *The Future of the Book,* ed. Goeffrey Nunberg, 24–26. Berkeley: University of California Press, 1996.

Jameson, Frederic. "The Ideology of the Text." *Salmagundi* 31/32 (1975/76): 204–46.

Johnson, Peggy. *Automation and Organizational Change in Libraries.* Boston: G. K. Hall, 1991.

Johnson, Peggy, and Bonnie MacEwan, eds. *Collection Management and Development: Issues in an Electronic Era.* ALCTS Papers on Library Technical Services and Collections, no. 5. Chicago: American Library Association, 1994.

———. "Copyright: An Introduction." *Library Acquisitions: Practice & Theory* 21, no. 1, (1997): 5–6.

Kanter, Rosabeth Moss. "Managing the Human Side of Change." *Management Review* 74 (April 1985): 52–56.

Kluegel, Kathleen. "Finding Our Way." *RQ* 36, no. 2 (winter 1996): 2–5.

———. "Redesigning Our Future." *RQ* 36, no. 3 (spring 1997): 2–6.

———. "The Reference Collection as Kaleidoscope." *RQ* 36, no. 1 (fall 1996): 2–4.

———. "Revolutionary Times." *RQ* 35, no. 4 (summer 1996): 1–3.

Kotter, John P. "Leading Change: Why Transformation Efforts Fail." *Harvard Business Review* 73 (1995): 603–31.

Kuhn, Thomas. *The Structure of Scientific Revolution.* 2nd ed. Chicago: University of Chicago Press, 1970.

Lagoze, Carl. "The Warwick Framework: A Container Architecture for Diverse Sets of Metadata." *D-Lib Magazine* (July/August 1996). http://www.dlib.org/july96/lagoze/07lagoze.html.

Lee, Catherine A. "The Changing Face of the College Student: The Impact of Generation X on Reference and Instructional Services." In *The Changing Face of Reference,* ed. Lynne M. Stuart and Dena Holiman Hutto, 107–18. Greenwich, Conn.: JAI Press, 1996.

Lehmann, Klaus-Dieter. "Making the Transitory Permanent: The Intellectual Heritage in a Digitized World of Knowledge." *Daedalus* 125 (fall 1996): 307–29.

Lenzer, Robert P., and Stephen S. Johnson. "Seeing Things As They Really Are." *Forbes* 159, no. 5 (1997): 122–28.

Levy, Amir. "Second-Order Planned Change: Definition and Conceptualization." *Organizational Dynamics* 15, no. 1 (summer 1986): 5–20.

Lewin, Kurt. "Frontiers in Group Dynamics: Concepts, Method, and Reality in Social Sciences: Social Equilibria and Social Change." *Human Relations* 1 (June 1947): 5–41.

Losee, Robert M. "A Discipline Independent Definition of Information." *Journal of the American Society for Information Science* 48 (March 1997): 254–69.

Lougee, Wendy P. "Beyond Access: New Concepts, New Tensions for Collection Development in a Digital Environment." *Collection Building* 14, no. 3 (1995): 19–25.

Lowry, Charles B. "Management Issues in the 'Infomated' Library." In *Information Management and Organizational Change in Higher Education: The Impact on Academic Libraries,* ed. Gary M. Pitkin, 100–131. Westport, Conn.: Meckler, 1992.

Lyman, Peter. "What Is a Digital Library? Technology, Intellectual Property, and the Public Interest." *Daedalus* 125 (fall 1996): 1–33.

Lynch, Clifford A. "Interoperability, Scaling, and the Digital Libraries' Research Agenda." *Microcomputers for Information Management* 13, no. 2 (1996): 85–131.

Lynch, Richard. "Creating Partnerships: Forging a Chain of Service Quality." *Journal of Library Administration* 18, no. 1–2 (1993): 137–55.

Marshak, Robert J. "Managing the Metaphors of Change." *Organizational Dynamics* 22 (1993): 44–56.

Marx, Karl. *Capital, the Communist Manifesto, and Other Writings,* ed. Max Eastman. New York: Modern Library, 1959.

"Metadata: An Overview." http://www.nla.gov.au/nla/staffpaper/cathro3.html/

Miller, Danny, and Peter Friesen. "Archetypes of Organizational Transition." *Administrative Science Quarterly* 25 (1980): 268–99.

Miller, Vernon D., John R. Johnson, and Jennifer Grau. "Antecedents to Willingness to Participate in a Planned Organizational Change." *Journal of Applied Communication Research* 22 (1994): 59–80.

Moore, Linda. "Getting Past the Rapids: Individuals and Change." *Serials Librarian* 25, no. 3/4 (1995): 95–109.

Moreland, Virginia. "Technostress and Personality Type." *Online* 17, no. 4 (July 1993): 59–62.

Nimmer, Melville B., and David Nimmer. *Nimmer on Copyright.* New York: Matthew Bender, 1997.

Okerson, Ann. "Copyright or Contract?" *Library Journal* 122 (September 1, 1997): 136–39.

Reuschlein, Harold Gill, and William A. Gregory. *The Law of Agency and Partnership.* 2nd ed. St. Paul, Minn.: West, 1990.

Schaffer, Robert H., and Harvey A. Thomson. "Successful Change Programs Begin with Results." *Harvard Business Review* 70 (1992): 80–89.

Schneider, Karen G. "Internet Librarian: A Nice Little Digital Library." *American Libraries* 28 (October 1997): 76.

Shapiro, James. "University Libraries: The 7-Per-Cent Solution." *Chronicle of Higher Education.* December 12, 1997, B 4–5.

Sheldon, Amy. "Organizational Paradigms: A Theory of Organizational Change." *Organizational Dynamics* 8 (winter 1980): 61–80.

St. Clair, Gloriana. "Restructuring and Benchmarking: Partners for Change." In *Restructuring Academic Libraries: Organization Development in the Wake of Technology Change,* ed. Charles A. Schwartz, 200–212. ACRL Publications in Librarianship, no. 49. Chicago: American Library Association, 1997.

Summerfield, Mary, Carol A. Mandel, and Paul Kantor. "Online Books at Columbia: Measurement and Early Results on Use, Satisfaction, and Effect: Interim Report of the Andrew W. Mellon Foundation-Funded Columbia

University Online Books Evaluation Project." Paper presented at the Scholarly Communication and Technology Conference, Emory University, Atlanta, Ga., April 24–25, 1997. http://www.arl.org/scomm/scat/summerfield. ind.html

Tichy, Noel M. "Managing Change Strategically: The Technical, Political, and Cultural Keys." *Organizational Dynamics* 11 (autumn 1982): 59–80.

Tryon, Jonathan S. *The Librarian's Legal Companion.* New York: G. K. Hall, 1994.

Tuckman, Bruce W. "Developmental Sequence in Small Groups." *Psychological Bulletin* 63, no. 6 (1965): 384–99.

Vaill, Peter B. *Learning as a Way of Being: Strategies for Survival in a World of Permanent White Water.* San Francisco: Jossey-Bass, 1996.

Young, Arthur P. "Information Technology and Libraries: A Virtual Convergence." *Cause-Effect* 17, no. 3 (1994): 5–6, 12.

Young, Peter. "Librarianship: A Changing Profession." *Daedalus* (fall 1996): 103–25.

Zemsky, Robert, and William F. Massy. "Expanding Perimeters, Melting Cores, and Sticky Functions: Toward an Understanding of Our Current Predicaments." *Change* 27 (1995): 41–49.

Acronyms

A&I	Abstracting and Indexing Databases
ALA	American Library Association
ALCTS	Association for Library Collections and Technical Services
ARPA	Advanced Research Projects Agency
CLIR	Council on Library and Information Resources
CLR	Council on Library Resources
EAD	Encoded Archival Description
FTP	File Transfer Protocol
IEE	Institute of Electrical Engineers
IEEE	Institute of Electrical and Electronics Engineers
IMS	Instructional Management System
IP Address	Internet Protocol Address
JSTOR	Journal Storage Project
LC	Library of Congress
MARC	MAchine Readable Cataloging

NASA	National Aeronautics and Space Administration
NLII	National Learning Infrastructure Initiative
NSF	National Science Foundation
OCLC	Online Computer Library Center
RITS	Research and Instructional Technology Support
RLG	Research Libraries Group
RUSA	Reference and User Services Association
SICI - SISAC	Serial Item Contribution Identifier - Serial Industry Systems Advisory Committee
SRRQ	Social Readjustment Rating Questionnaire
UCC	Uniform Commerical Code
URL	Uniform Resource Locator
URN	Uniform Resource Name

Contributors

Ross Atkinson is Deputy University Librarian at Cornell University, where he is responsible for the coordination of service operations throughout the Cornell Library system. Before moving to Cornell in 1988, he was Assistant University Librarian for Collection Development at the University of Iowa. He is a member of the Planning Task Force of the Digital Library Federation. His more recent publications include the articles "Library Functions, Scholarly Communication, and the Foundation of the Digital Library," *Library Quarterly* 66 (July 1996): 239–65; "Access, Ownership and the Future of Collection Development," in *Collection Management and Development* (American Library Association, 1994); and "Humanities Scholarship and the Research Library," *Library Resources & Technical Services* 39 (January 1995): 79–84.

Kenneth Crews is an associate professor at the Indiana University School of Law and in the School of Library and Information Science, as well as Director of the Copyright Management Center in Indianapolis and a regular participant in the Conference on Fair Use. His principal research interest has been the relationship of copyright law to the needs of higher education. His most recent book is *Copyright, Fair Use, and the Challenge for Universities: Promoting the Progress of Higher Education* (University of Chicago Press, 1993).

Trisha Davis is an assistant professor and Head of the Continuation Acquisition Division at the Ohio State University Libraries. She has taught graduate courses in technical services and cataloging for Kent State School of Library and Information Science since 1987. She has developed a two-day workshop on licensing for the Association of Research Libraries (ARL) that is being presented across the country, and she has written a book on automated serial control systems. She also consults for businesses and libraries on projects related to the licensing of electronic products.

Kenneth Dowlin has devoted thirty-five years to building community support for library facilities and services. In each of five different libraries, he managed to increase the budget by at least 100 percent. He has been active in library associations at all levels, and is a past chair of the Colorado Library Association, as well as of LITA and many other library committees. The publication of *The Electronic Library: The Promise and the Process* (Neal-Schuman, 1984) established Dowlin at the forefront of library implementation of electronic technology. He has published many dozens of articles and spoken all over the nation and the world.

John Howe is a history professor at the University of Minnesota, where he also served for two years as interim University Librarian. His teaching and research interests focus on U.S. history. His library service includes terms on the board of governors of the Research Libraries Group and the Advisory Committee of the National Commission on Preservation and Access. He has been a frequent panelist for library and archives preservation and access projects for the National Endowment for the Humanities.

Peggy Johnson is Assistant University Librarian for the University of Minnesota Libraries. She has held a number of positions at the University of Minnesota, including Assistant Director, Saint Paul Campus Libraries; Interim Collection Development Planning Officer for the University of Minnesota Libraries; Interim Director, Saint Paul Campus Libraries; and Head of Technical Services, St. Paul Campus Libraries. Previously she worked for the University of Iowa Libraries, the St. Paul Public Library, and Control Data. A prolific writer, editor and speaker, her publications include the *Guide to Technical Services Resources* (1994) and *New Directions in Technical Services* (1997), both published by ALA. Johnson writes a bimonthly column on collection development in the journal *Technicalities*. She is an active member of the American Library Association and the Association for Library Collections and Technical Services. She has served on the ALCTS Board of Directors, Collection Management and Development Section Executive Board, the CMDS Continuing Education and Program Committee, and the CMDS Collection Development and Electronic Media Committee. She has been elected President of ALCTS for the 1999/2000 term.

Clifford Lynch is the Executive Director of the Coalition for Networked Information. He was formerly Director of Library Automation at the University of California Office of the President and was a leader in the development of the Melvyl system, which serves all the University system campuses. A specialty of his is networked information, a subject on which he has done extensive research and writing. He worked on the development of the Z39.50 standards for interoperability among information systems and served on the Board of Directors of the National Information Standards Organization. He is a past president of the American Society for Information Science.

Bonnie MacEwan is Assistant Dean for Collections at the Pennsylvania State University Libraries. She was chair of the Collection Development Committee at the University of Missouri for several years while holding the position of Art, Archaeology and Music Librarian. She has been active in ALCTS as a member of the planning committee for the Canadian Collection Management and Development Institute and cochair of the Advanced Collection Management and Development Institute, and in RUSA as chair of the Computer-Based Methods and Resources Committee and section secretary. She has written articles on several topics, including electronic journals and wired faculty, and with Peggy Johnson edited *Collection Management and Development: Issues in an Electronic Era* (American Library Association, 1994).

Deanna Marcum is president of a newly created nonprofit organization, the Council on Library and Information Resources (CLIR), formed by the merger of the Commission on Preservation and Access and the Council on Library Resources with the mission of identifying the critical issues that affect the welfare and prospects of libraries and archives and the constituencies they serve; convening individuals and organizations to respond to these issues; and encouraging institutions to work collaboratively to achieve and manage change. She has been Director of Public Service and Collection Management at the Library of Congress, Dean of the Catholic University of America School of Library and Information Sciences, and a vice president of the Council on Library Resources.

Kären Nagy is the Deputy University Librarian at Stanford University, where her responsibilities include delivery of the library's public services programs as well as many of the university's front line academic computing and instructional technology services. She began her library career as a music librarian at Northwestern University from 1975 to 1986. She was head of the Music Library and Archive of Recorded Sound at Stanford from 1986 to 1990 before moving into a senior administrative role there. Kären continues to hold a lecturer appointment in Stanford's Music Department and has also worked as a consultant in areas of library organizational change and library building design.

Karen Schmidt is Director of Collections and Assessment at the University of Illinois/Urbana-Champaign. She previously worked there as head of Library Acquisitions for fifteen years. Before coming to the UIUC Library, she worked at Ohio State University and Illinois State University. Schmidt has written extensively on library acquisitions, collections issues, serials cancellations, and library history. She also teaches collection development at the library school on the Urbana campus.

Gloriana St. Clair is University Librarian at Carnegie Mellon University. Previously she was Associate Dean and Head of Information Access Services at Penn State University, where she has also served as Interim Dean and Interim Associate Dean for Planning and Administrative Services. Before moving to Penn State, she was an administrator at Oregon State and Texas A&M University Libraries. She is the author of numerous scholarly articles, has edited *College & Research Libraries,* and currently is editor of the *Journal of Academic Librarianship.*

Eugene Wiemers has been College Librarian and a member of the Information Services Management Team at Bates College since 1994. Before that, he was Assistant University Librarian for Collection Management at Northwestern University, and has served in administrative roles in collection development and public services at Michigan State University and the University of Minnesota. A principal focus of his work has been the development of collaborative efforts among libraries. He helped plan cooperative projects in collection development and preservation among the Big Ten schools in his work for the Committee on Institutional Cooperation (CIC).

Index